Successful OSS Project Design and Implementation

Successful OSS Project Design and Implementation

Requirements, Tools, Social Designs and Reward Structures

Edited By
HIND BENBYA AND NASSIM BELBALY

Routledge
Taylor & Francis Group

LONDON AND NEW YORK

First published 2011 by Gower Publishing

Published 2016 by Routledge
2 Park Square, Milton Park, Abingdon, Oxon OX14 4RN
711 Third Avenue, New York, NY 10017, USA

Routledge is an imprint of the Taylor & Francis Group, an informa business

British Library Cataloguing in Publication Data
Successful OSS project design and implementation :
  requirements, tools, social designs and reward structures.
  1. Open source software. 2. Computer software--
  Development--Management.
  I. Benbya, Hind. II. Belbaly, Nassim.
  005.3-dc22

Library of Congress Cataloging-in-Publication Data
Benbya, Hind.
  Successful OSS project design and implementation : requirements, tools, social designs and
  reward structures / by Hind Benbya and Nassim Belbaly.
    p. cm.
  Includes index.
  ISBN 978-0-566-08795-0 (hbk) -- ISBN 978-1-4094-0957-1
  (ebook) 1. Open source software. 2. Computer software--Development. 3. Management
  information systems. 4. Information technology projects. I. Belbaly, Nassim. II. Title.
  QA76.76.S46B46 2010
  005.3--dc22

                                                                                                2010021054

ISBN 13: 978-0-566-08795-0 (hbk)

Contents

List of Figures

List of Tables

About the Editors

Hind Benbya is an associate professor of Information Technology (IT) management at GSCM-Montpellier Business School, France. Her research consists in developing frameworks and tools for implementing and evaluating complex IT (i.e., knowledge management systems, internal knowledge markets and co-creation communities).

Her publications appeared in different journals including, *MIT Sloan Management Review, Information Technology* and *People and Journal of Information Technology*. She is author of a book entitled *Knowledge Management Systems Implementation: Lessons from the Silicon Valley*.

Hind holds a PhD in electronic business management and two Master degrees. She has collaborated with leading organizations in Europe and the US and has been teaching, conducting research and consulting in several countries including the US, Switzerland, Italy and France.

Nassim Belbaly is an associate professor and dean of academic affairs at GSCM-Montpellier Business School, France. His areas of research interests include knowledge management and new product development. He is author of several articles published in peer-reviewed journals and book chapters. Dr Belbaly serves as a KM minitrack co-chair at the Hawaii International Conference on System Sciences.

Preface

Over the last decade, open source software – software that can be freely used, modified and redistributed – has emerged as a mode for developing and organizing software innovation. The exchange of software code among developers was the norm at the beginning of the computer industry, when much of the software was developed in-house by scientists and engineers of university departments and corporate research laboratories. But this practice slowly disappeared and proprietary software emerged as the dominant paradigm.

Today, the open source phenomenon has attracted an increased interest among commercial firms and governments and is becoming one of the most influential paradigm shifts not only in software development but in social and economic value creation as well.

While software development is perhaps the most prominent example of open source, its principles have been applied across a wide range of product classes, industries and even scientific disciplines. Some of these principles can be summarized as follows:

1. *A voluntary association of actors*, typically lacking *a priori* common organizational affiliation (i.e. not working for the same firm) but united by a shared instrumental goal – in this case, creating, adapting, adopting or disseminating software.

2. *Self-organization*, where individual developers construct communities on the Internet through large-scale collaboration and information sharing.

3. *Self-sustainment* as the majority of open source projects (OSP) doesn't rely on any corporate or commercial sponsorship.

4.   *Co-creation*, which often results in value creation that becomes customized products or services.

As a consequence, there is an increasing interest in understanding the structure and development of these communities and how they create value.

This collection of chapters provides a state-of-the-art analysis of the open source software design principles, their emergence and success and how they are extending well beyond the domain of software. The authors examine a number of fundamental issues in this area. These include a brief history of open source emergence from communities of developers to firms and governmental organizations, examining how these communities organize, comparing their model to other domains, explaining what we know about their motives to take part and contribute to such projects, exploring the potential of several incentives schemes, analysing their success factors and metrics and how they have been applied so far; and, finally, laying out a research agenda to help improve our understanding of successful open source software projects and how we might apply its principles in other domains beyond software.

Introduction

Successful OSS Project (OSSP) Design and Implementation is organized in three parts. Each part is designed to respond to a key question and is composed of three chapters.

Part I: OSS Emergence and Development provides a brief history on the open source movement, its development and how its principles have shifted from communities of developers to firms, governmental organizations and several other domains.

Part II: OSS Rewards' and Incentives' Structure discusses the intriguing question of why so many developers dedicate time and effort to contributing to open source projects (OSP). It provides an analysis of motivation from an individual developer and a community perspective, and suggests a credit system as an alternative scheme to the current incentives structure.

Part III: OSS Success, Measurement and Metrics answers the question of how we can measure the success of OSSP. It describes several measures of OSSP effectiveness and how to operationalize them, analyses important success factors in the context of OSS and investigates the case of small and active projects on SourceForge.

Part I: OSS Emergence and Development

After a brief summary of OSS history, its emergence and extension into other domains, Lakhani and Panetta (Chapter 1) characterize the principles behind OSS communities' organization and success. They describe OSS communities as the most significant model of distributed innovation systems, and provide an overview of how this model is applied in three different industries, specifically software development (Linux), T-shirt design (Threadless) and research and development (Innocentive). They then characterize their main differences, analyse the motivations of participants and discuss organizational and intellectual property issues raised by this new mode of organizing work. They conclude with a discussion on the main challenges and limits of these communities.

In Chapter 2, Bonaccorci et al. analyse whether and how firms get involved, to various extents, in the OSS movement. They first provide a brief evolution of firms' participation in OSP. Then, they provide empirical evidence on the role and activities of software companies in community developed projects. Using a large-scale primary data collection from OSS project repositories and linked websites, they show how today's OSS movement differs from its origins and how firms' involvement has become important, not only in terms of increased participation but also in terms of OSS's impact on community projects.

In Chapter 3, Rentocchini and Tartari survey OSS adoption by the public sector in the Emilia-Romagna region. Emilia-Romagna is an Italian region that has recently been characterized by strong commitments towards e-government investments and is among a few regions in Europe to be provided with a public administration broadband infrastructure connecting the whole territory. The authors integrate their survey of information systems' division managers in public administrations with collected data from a European Union project data. Results from their investigation characterize OSS software types and applications adopted by public administrations, and describe strengths and limits related to free/libre open source software (FLOSS) adoption by local governments. They conclude by providing tentative policy recommendations for FLOSS adoption.

Part II: OSS Rewards' and Incentives' Structure

First, Benbya (Chapter 4) summarizes the literature on motivation of developers in OSP analysing the reasons put forward by three different disciplines – economic, sociology and psychology – to explain developers' involvement in such projects. She then integrates constructs from psychology and social exchange theories to develop a theoretical model relating antecedents and outcomes of OSS developers' behaviour. The model is tested through an empirical survey of OSS developers using SourceForge.

Following this, Robey and Wang (Chapter 5) present a cross-level theoretical model to analyse the role of community-level social capital in individual-level contributions to OSS projects. Social capital is proposed to moderate the relationship between individual motivation and individual contributions. A high level of social capital in an OSS community can strengthen the relationship between motivation and contribution, whereas a low-level of social capital can weaken that relationship. The propositions of the model are developed using secondary published sources describing OSS projects, especially the case of the Apache web server project.

Finally, Barwolff (Chapter 6) puts forward an alternative incentive scheme based on the notion of a credit framework and discusses its potential and limits within the context of OSSP. He argues that credits have a high redemption potential in that they may buy things that plain money cannot. On the other hand, however, the scope of potential redemption for credits obtained in free software development is by no means as broad as that of money credits, making for inefficiencies both in the incentive structure and the way in which free software projects may interface with more money-oriented contexts.

Part III: OSS Success, Measurement and Metrics

Stewart (Chapter 7), using a multi-dimensional conceptualization of success, including both a development and a usage perspective, summarizes findings from three studies on success factors in OSS. The first study focuses mainly on the influence of three kinds of team factors on development success measures. The second study explores how a project factor, development status, moderates the relationships among the team factors in study one and different measures of development success. The third study focuses mainly on the role that project factors, licence restrictiveness and project sponsorship, have on both development success and usage success. The chapter concludes by discussing research in progress to build on the findings in these three studies and to explore the impact of user factors.

Following this, Crowston and Howison (Chapter 8) analyse the success of open source software by focusing on project success of one of the most widely used dependent variables in information systems research. They discuss how conventional measures of project success are difficult to apply to FLOSS and present an analysis of four commonly used measures of success applied to SourceForge projects: number of developers, posters to discussion boards, number of downloads and number of page views. They argue that these four measures provide different insights on project effectiveness and illustrate their analysis with an example to compare different projects.

Finally, Rainer and Gale (Chapter 9) investigate the success of very small and active projects on SourceForge. They compare how these projects differ from large projects usually studied in SourceForge and provide several suggestions for defining and studying their success.

PART I

OSS Emergence and Development

Over the past decade, there has been a phenomenal increase in the adoption of open source software (OSS) by both firms and governments. OS is largely recognized today as an alternative way of developing and distributing software of high quality with relatively lower costs. Today, many large multinational firms such as IBM, HP and Sun Microsystems, to name just a few examples, dedicate substantial resources and sponsor developers to contribute to OSSP.

Even Microsoft, which has traditionally been hostile to the entire open source model, now realizes that important technological innovations can be developed in conjunction with the open source community. Recently, the company has assigned formal executive responsibilities for open source strategy and has established a staff to assist with outbound and inbound open source software. Yet, the entire OSS movement is a product of technologically oriented individuals primarily motivated by goals other than economic.

The free/open source movement initially started in the 1970s as a kind of ideology against proprietary software, campaigning for users' freedom and for making all software free of intellectual property restrictions. This movement has evolved considerably in recent years. It's still working towards most of the same ideological values; however, it takes a much more pragmatic approach advancing the economic and technical merits of OSS over its moral or ethical principles. Lately, with the increasing number of companies sponsoring OSSP, it has become clear that this movement is taking a new path with some even predicting its shift to a commercial product.

In this part, the three chapters provide a different but complementary view on the evolution of the OSS movement. The first chapter, *Principles of Distributed Innovation*, illustrates the principles characterizing OSS communities and how they have been applied to other domains. The second chapter, *Firms' Participation in FOSS*, describes how OSS has evolved from communities of developers to firms and how firms participate in different ways to OSSP.

Chapter 3, *OSS in the Public Sector*, summarizes the results of a survey on OSS adoption by public administrations in Emilia-Romagna.

1

The Principles of Distributed Innovation

Karim Lakhani and Jill Panetta

"No matter who you are, most of the smartest people work for someone else" is known as Joy's Law in the high-tech industry. Attributed to Sun Microsystems cofounder Bill Joy, this "law" emphasizes the essential knowledge problem that faces many enterprises today; that is, that in any given sphere of activity most of the pertinent knowledge will reside outside the boundaries of any one organization, and the central challenge for those charged with the innovation mission is to find ways to access that knowledge.

The causal explanation of Joy's Law is provided in the seminal work of economists Friedrich Hayek and Eric von Hippel on the distributed and sticky nature of knowledge and innovation. Hayek (1945), arguing for the importance of the market economy, emphasized that at the macro level knowledge is unevenly distributed in society, and that centralized models for economic planning and coordination are prone to failure due to an inability to aggregate this distributed knowledge. Thirty years later, micro-level studies by von Hippel (2005) began to suggest that in many industries users were the originators of most novel innovations. Users' dominant role in originating innovations reflects the fact that knowledge is not only distributed but also "sticky," that is, relatively difficult and extremely costly to move between locations, thus shifting the locus of innovation to where it is the stickiest (von Hippel 1994). Users generate functionally novel innovations because they experience novel needs well ahead of manufacturers, and manufacturers develop dimension of merit innovations (that improve the performance of existing features) because they specialize in producing products for the mass market.[1] Joy's Law is

---

1   See Riggs and von Hippel (1994) for an analysis showing how novel functionality emerges from users.

exacerbated by the explosion of knowledge in most scientific and technological fields. In the online database of the US National Library of Medicine (Medline), for example, between 1955 and 2005, the number of academic papers published in the life sciences increased approximately six-and-one-half-fold, from 105,000 to 686,000.[2] Even in relatively narrow and obscure fields, tissue engineering for instance, 6,131 academic publications were authored by 17,044 individuals between 2004 and 2006.[3] In the face of this explosion of knowledge, most organizations will have difficulty keeping up with significant trends and identifying and locking up key sources of knowledge for competitive gain. Joy's Law is thus not so much a statement about the declining IQs of workers or poor hiring practices as an acknowledgement that the traditionally closed models of proprietary innovation will have difficulty completing knowledge-intensive tasks when most of the needed knowledge resides outside the organization. The successful development of the Linux operating system and numerous other open source software (OSS) projects provides an alternative model for organizing for innovation. Many practitioners and scholars of innovation did not anticipate the emergence of a distributed and open model for innovation that can aggressively compete with traditionally closed and proprietary models. That complex software systems running mission critical applications can be designed, developed, maintained, and improved for "free" by a virtual "community" of mostly volunteer computer programmers has come as a great surprise to them. Perhaps even more surprising is that some of the largest software companies and the biggest holders of intellectual property (for example, IBM, Sun, Apple, and Oracle) have embraced OSS communities by encouraging the participation of their own personnel in, and donating copyrighted software and patents to, these communities, and integrating OSS software into their strategic product and service offerings.

OSS communities are the most fully developed example of the appearance of distributed innovation systems characterized by decentralized problem solving, self-selected participation, self-organizing coordination and collaboration, "free" revealing of knowledge, and hybrid organizational models that blend community with commercial success. The achievements of OSS communities have brought the distributed innovation model to general attention, but it is rapidly taking hold in industries as diverse as apparel and clothing, encyclopedias, biotechnology and pharmaceuticals, and music and entertainment.

---

2   Data obtained by searching on this website http://dan.corlan.net/cgi-bin/medline-trend?Q=,accessed on September 16, 2007.
3   Analysis done by Intellectual Property Practice of The Boston Consulting Group.

In this chapter, we first provide an overview of distributed innovation systems that are achieving success in three different industries with three different organizational models. We then consider in the context of these three examples questions and concerns related to why people participate, the organizing principles of production, and the implications for intellectual property. We close our discussion with a review of potential extensions and limitations of this alternative model of innovation.

Models for Distributed Innovation

THE SELF-ORGANIZING COMMUNITY

Linux invariably comes to mind when OSS communities are mentioned. Its organizational and commercial success has stunned most observers. Linux's growth from just over 10,000 lines of code at its inception to about four million lines of code as of the latest version reflects the contributions of thousands of individuals (Amor-Iglesias et al. 2005). In 2007, 1,961 developers added 754,000 lines of code.[4] The commercial ecosystem that surrounds Linux was expected to reach about US$35 billion in 2008 with installations in more than 43 million computing devices ranging from PCs and servers to cell phones, routers, DVRs and super computer clusters.[5] Its beginnings belie the contemporary scope and value of this global movement. Linux's genesis in 1991, in the pre-Web era of the Internet, was a series of announcements and requests for help posted by then 22-year-old Linus Torvalds on a message board for computer operating systems.[6]

> *Hello netlanders, Do you pine for the nice days of minix-1.1, when men were men and wrote their own device drivers? Are you without a nice project and just dying to cut your teeth on an OS you can try to modify for your needs? … :-)*

> *I'm doing a (free) operating system, just a hobby, won't be big and professional… I'd like any feedback on things people like/dislike … This is a program for hackers by a hacker. I've enjoyed doing it, and somebody*

---

4   See http://lwn.net/Articles/222773/, accessed on September 16, 2007.
5   See   http://www.techweb.com/wire/showArticle.jhtml?articleID=55800522,   accessed   on September 16, 2007.
6   Text shows messages sent to the comp.os.minix Usenet group between July and October 1991.

might enjoy looking at it and even modifying it for their own needs ...
Drop me a line if you are willing to let me use your code.
                              Linus (torvalds@kruuna.helsinki.fi)

These announcements set in motion a loose, informal collaboration that led to the establishment of a framework for interaction among the global community of software developers that created the Linux kernel (the core of a computer operating system). As Torvalds' messages make clear, the initial drivers of participation in Linux were user need and fun. The promise of Linux was of a powerful Unix-like operating system, previously available only on high-end hardware that could run on commodity Intel hardware. Because it was available on the Internet, users could download the source code to their own computers and modify it to suit their needs and interests. Modifications made to the source code were then sent back to Torvalds in the hope that they would be included in the next release of the kernel. The growing community established its own Internet-based discussion forums and began to work collaboratively to resolve technical issues related to Linux development. Although over the past 16 years the number of people and firms interested in Linux has continued to grow, the basic model of participation on the basis of user need or curiosity and having fun has not changed. To participate one need only sign up for the Linux kernel mailing list (LKML) and be competent to modify source code. LKML is the rendezvous point for technical discussions of the features being developed by contributors. LKML participants report and fix bugs, contribute and modify code, and discuss the technical evolution of the kernel.

Although Torvalds has final say as to what goes into the kernel, much of the development is organic, determined by the actions of community members and not by any measure of explicit project management within the community. Torvalds' philosophy regarding management of the community runs counter to most expectations of how complex technological projects should be run. A recent debate within LKML highlights the issues.[7]

Rik van Riel (an active contributor to Linux):

> *"It seems like Linux really isn't going anywhere in particular and seems to make progress through sheer luck."*

---

7   See Lakhani and Wolf (2005) for an overview of findings on motivations to participate in open source communities.

Linus Torvalds (in several emails in a longer thread):

"Hey, that's not a bug, that's a FEATURE

Well, sheer luck, AND:

- *free availability and crosspollination through sharing of 'source code,' although biologists call it DNA.*
- *a rather unforgiving user environment, that happily replaces bad versions of us with better working versions and thus culls the herd (biologists often call this 'survival of the fittest')*
- *massive undirected parallel development ('trial and error')*

Do I direct some stuff? Yes. But, quite frankly, so do many others. Alan, Al, David, even you. And a lot of companies are part of the evolution whether they realize it or not. And all the users end up being part of the 'fitness testing'...

A strong vision and a sure hand sound good on paper. It's just that I have never met a technical person (including me) whom I would trust to know what is really the right thing to do in the long run...

Too strong a strong vision can kill you — you'll walk right over the edge firm in the knowledge of the path in front of you...

I'd much rather have 'brownian motion,' where a lot of microscopic directed improvements end up pushing the system slowly in a direction that none of the individual developers really had the vision to see on their own. And I'm a firm believer that in order for this to work well, you have to have a development group that is fairly strange and random."

Most managers would balk at developing complex technological artifacts with the help of "fairly strange and random" individuals. But Torvalds and Linux show the potential benefit of organizing work such that many individuals can self-select and lead elements of development without much ex-ante guidance and control.

BLENDING COMMUNITY AND COMMERCE

Threadless.com foreshadows the commercial enterprise of the future, that is, built to leverage community-based distributed innovation. Firms in the apparel and fashion business face two critical challenges:

1.   to attract the right designer talent at the right time to create recurring fashion hits, and

2.   to forecast sales so as to be better able to match production cycles with demand cycles.

Threadless solves these problems by letting its international community of customers take over such core functions as innovation, new product development, sales forecasting, and marketing.

Threadless was started in 2000 by childhood friends Jake Nickell and Jacob DeHart who were active participants in a Chicago-based online community of designers called Dreamless. The experience of winning a T-shirt design competition sponsored by the Dreamless community exposed Nickell, and by association his friend DeHart, to the idea that co-creation with a community was a relatively untapped market. Both were amazed by the variety and high quality of submissions received by the community organizers. As budding designers, they realized early on that the fashion industry was fickle and they had no monopoly on good design ideas. But a platform that solicited design ideas from anyone and provided for community-based selection of submitted designs might overcome their own limitations. Hence Threadless was formed. Threadless.com's business model revolves around an ongoing competition to which anyone, professional graphic designers and amateurs alike, can submit designs for new T-shirts. The community is polled on both the designs (which are rated using a scale of zero to five) and willingness to buy. Threadless uses this information to select for production six to 10 new designs each week. Winning designs' creators receive cash and prizes worth US$2,500, are recognized for their accomplishment on the company's website, and have their screen name printed on the T-shirt label. Community members also critique submitted designs and provide feedback to help designers improve their ideas going forward. Threadless also populates its online catalog with photographs of community members wearing T-shirts bearing winning designs. Threadless has become both a commercial and community success story. In 2006, it sold more than 1.5 million T-shirts to customers around the world, and its active community exceeds 600,000 members. Threadless receives more than 800 new design submissions per week, each of which is typically rated and assigned a demand signal indicating intent to purchase by more than 1,500 community members. More than half of purchasers have, at one time or another, voted on T-shirt designs. The online community is vibrant, logging in excess of 500 new member posts per day discussing design and art and submitting music and video inspired by designs. All of this has been accomplished with little or no reliance on traditional forms of advertising and customer recruitment. Such has been its success that the company has on many occasions declined overtures by large-scale retailers to sell Threadless T-shirts in stores around the world.

GETTING OUTSIDERS TO INNOVATE

InnoCentive.com is changing how the toughest science-based research and development (R&D) problems get solved by traditionally closed enterprises in the pharmaceutical, biotechnology, consumer goods, and high-technology industries. The business offers firms that encounter difficult science problems an alternative to devoting laboratory time and resources to the search for a solution. Firms can now post such problems, together with a designated cash prize (typically ranging from US$5,000 to US$100,000) for an acceptable solution, on InnoCentive.com. Problem posters and prospective solvers, who self-select to the attempt to devise or formulate a solution, remain anonymous to one another throughout the process. InnoCentive's role is that of knowledge broker, providing the seeker firms that post problems with solutions solvers have been motivated to submit. The seeker firm chooses the most appropriate solution, if any, and receives from the solver, in return for the prize money, all rights to the intellectual property related to the solution. InnoCentive was spun off from Eli Lilly and Company's Internet incubator in 2000. The driver of InnoCentive was then-vice president of R&D Alph Bingham, who recalled from his doctoral student days that most science problems were potentially amenable to multiple approaches and diverse solutions, and that often top students in one problem area were not necessarily at the top in another. Yet, within firms, he realized, science problems were typically assigned to a single scientist or a small team possibly either not at the top in the problem domain or unaware of alternative approaches. Having seen his share of projects and problems being tackled internally that had gotten stuck or lain fallow because solutions were not forthcoming, Bingham reasoned that a dedicated company that could connect diverse "outside" scientists with "inside" problems could be the answer to some of the scientific productivity challenges in pharmaceuticals and other industries. InnoCentive's solver network includes more than 120,000 scientists from around the world. More than 400 problems that could not be solved by the R&D laboratories of some 50 firms have been posted. Each problem piques the interest of more than 200 scientists, about 10 of whom submit solutions. About one-third of the problems posted by seeker firms have been solved and the associated prizes awarded. Solutions arrive from unexpected sources and are typically not what the originating problem holder scientists had envisioned as possible. For example, one firm had experienced difficulty transferring a chemical powder to a specialty container. Whereas most of the unsuccessful solutions proposed within the firm had attempted to enable transport by modifying the material's chemical properties, the winning solution submitted by an InnoCentive solver employed instead the use of electrostatic charge, in essence, applying a physics solution to a chemistry problem.

In another case, an aerospace physicist, a small agribusiness owner, a transdermal drug delivery specialist, and an industrial scientist all submitted diverse winning solutions to the same scientific problem: identification of a polymer delivery system.

Motivations to Participate

"Why do people work and participate for 'free'?" is one of the first questions asked when distributed innovation systems are encountered. The emergence of OSS communities and sheer numbers of participants, in the hundreds of thousands, raised the question of motivation in distributed innovation. Certainly, the common view of "homo economicus," of purely self-interested participants, is not the answer when many participate with no promise of a direct financial reward for their efforts. The answer lies rather in a more expansive view that acknowledges, as well as the role of narrow economic motivations, notions of enjoyment and having fun together with identity and the social benefits of community.

Research on OSS communities has shown motivation to participate to breakout broadly into extrinsic—that is, direct or indirect rewards for performing a task—and intrinsic—that is, valuing a task for its own sake. In the context of OSS, participation is driven primarily by user need. Programmers observe that they contribute time, effort, and intellect because they have a direct need for a particular software functionality that is not available from commercial sources. That individuals participate because they can use the software and features to which they have directly contributed for work or non-work purposes is consistent with the fact that approximately 40 per cent of the participants in OSS communities are paid to participate. Employees are encouraged by their employers to contribute code to OSS communities because software that addresses needs of the organization might result through community development. In the case of output that is not needed by the contributor, a cash reward might be tendered for substantial contributions. Such efforts are not undertaken with any ex-ante guarantee that they will be rewarded. Rather, payment is at the discretion of the sponsoring organization, made after the work has been completed and evaluated as meeting a certain criteria, and is usually attended by the formal transfer of intellectual property between contributor and sponsor.

Beyond pecuniary benefits, extrinsic reasons for participation include job market signaling and skill and reputation building. Distributed innovation communities provide a relatively open and transparent platform for exhibiting skills and talents to prospective employers. Participants don't need high-level credentials to directly demonstrate their abilities in highly specialized domains, and employers can screen and hire talent by directly observing or soliciting third-party verification of skills. Peer review benefits both members and products. The experience of the community can be leveraged both to improve the quality of contributions and to provide skill-enhancing feedback to contributors. Participants' open activities also accrue reputation among peers. Consistently contributing top-notch code and helping to bring along other members of the community earn status that often translates into privileges within and reputation outside the community, with the attendant possibility of future rewards. If writing code, designing graphic elements, and solving tough science problems are construed by outsiders to be unremunerated blood, sweat, and tears, the contributors themselves are more likely to insist that the work is a source of significant satisfaction that derives from the pure joy of engagement in the work, or with the group or community, or both. Research has shown that members of OSS communities quite simply enjoy the programming task sufficiently to want to devote their incremental free time to it.

Programming has been observed to put some in a "flow state" whereby enjoyment of the task is maximized and intense and focused concentration is achieved.[8] A flow state results when a person's skill matches the challenge of a task. A task beyond an individual's skill provokes anxiety; a task beneath an individual's skill induces boredom. Achieving a flow state also correlates with

---

8   See Csikszentmihalyi (1990) for an excellent overview of how work can be fun and satisfying in a wide range of professions.

a personal sense of creativity. A majority of respondents in OSS communities report their involvement in various software projects to be among the most creative work they've undertaken in their lives. Challenge, enjoyment, and creativity are hallmarks of "voluntary" participation in distributed innovation. Similar findings regarding the importance of the intellectual challenge and enjoyment of the task at hand have been reported on the part of InnoCentive solvers and Threadless designers.

A strong sense of identity and community belonging also motivates participation. Individuals who strive to be active players in the community are inclined to act in a manner consistent with its norms. Contributors are socialized by their participation into acting in a way that advances the collective. For example, because the norms of free revealing and code sharing are universally accepted and expected in OSS communities, many participate openly. Members who have benefited personally from using source code developed by many other members, moreover, feel obliged to give back to their community. Finally, OSS communities can be a source of a sense of self-identity that can lead members to undertake tasks that benefit the community generally. This sense of belonging, which has been observed as well in communities formed by firms, has been found to be quite powerful. The intrinsic and extrinsic motivations to participate in distributed innovation systems are not intuitively obvious to new observers of the phenomenon. Most, in fact, find to be counterintuitive the association of fun, enjoyment, and a personal sense of identity with the accomplishment of complex technical tasks. But the research findings strongly suggest that the functioning of these systems is driven by mixed and heterogeneous motivations. Consequently, optimizing on only one dimension might have the effect of limiting participation.

Organizing Principles

"Brownian motion-based management" is not yet taught in any business schools. But the participation of commercial enterprises in OSS communities and other distributed innovation systems suggest that organizing principles for participation, collaboration, and self-organization can be distilled. Importantly, these systems are not "managed" in the traditional sense of the word; that is, "smart" managers are not recruiting staff, offering incentives for hard work, dividing tasks, integrating activities, and developing career paths. Rather, the locus of control and management lies with the individual participants who decide themselves the terms of interaction with each other.

Key to participation is contributors' self-selection to tasks. In the case of OSS, contributors self-select to tasks that will generate functionality that they need or eliminate a bug that is hindering their use of functionality that is otherwise available to them. Self-selection to tasks can also be influenced by what other community members are indicating to be potential issues and opportunities. But whatever the driver, the matching of individuals' skills and tasks at hand is entirely at the discretion of the individual contributors. Rarely do community "managers" allocate tasks or attempt to perform this matching. InnoCentive contributors similarly self-select to science problems for which they perceive a match between their knowledge base and abilities and the requirements of the solution, and the designs submitted to Threadless reflect contributors' individual interests, inspirations, and graphic design skills. Furthermore, Carliss Baldwin and Kim Clark have shown how "the architecture of participation" in distributed innovation systems is driven by the granularity and diversity of the tasks available in a given context.[9] The more granular and diverse the available tasks, the larger the potential pool of participants. Participation in Threadless, for example, is not limited to individuals with bona fide graphic design skills. Non-designers can provide feedback, suggest changes in color and graphical elements, for example, and also indicate their preferences for and willingness to purchase particular designs, contributions that are as essential to the success of the business as the submission of designs. There is also an important role in the grass roots marketing of the business and community that is played by those who contribute digital photographs and videos of themselves wearing Threadless T-shirts, and post to the site's lively blog.

The task granularity and diversity observed in OSS communities is reflected in the range of opportunities open to contributors, who not only might update existing as well as write new code, but also report or fix bugs, request new features, engage in discussions of approaches to coding, write documentation, create and improve graphical user interfaces, translate interfaces into different languages, and provide user-to-user technical support. Tasks generally remain latent until they pique the interest of a contributor with the requisite skills. Core members of OSS communities, often possessing use experience in narrow domains, rely on other participants to help identify and then fulfill the missing elements. Even in the case of the problems posted on InnoCentive, the solutions to most of which might be expected to be formulated by individuals with advanced scientific training, granularity is important. The problems posted are not of infinite scope, "finding a cure for cancer or discovering anti-gravity," for

---

9   See Baldwin and Clark (2006) for a very novel analysis of how code structure can impact community participation.

example, but rather are sufficiently decomposed to accommodate attempts by individual scientists to solve them using locally available materials, methods, and tools.

Granularity also helps to assure that solvers will not devote inordinate amounts of time to attempts to devise solutions that ultimately prove unsuccessful.

Task granularity and diversity in distributed innovation systems are further enhanced by the information processing nature of most tasks and widespread availability of low cost tools that support innovation.[10] OSS communities emerged as an ideal type of distributed innovation system because the functionality required for software invention, innovation, production, and distribution are digital and information-based. The tools required for software production—text editors, compilers, debuggers, and source code repositories—are widely available and cheap (in most instances, even free). The high degree of fidelity with respect to error detection and correction provided by these tools enables contributors to share and evaluate each others' as well as newcomers' contributions. The efficacy of assertions about software designs and operations is quickly proved by the requirement that they can be converted into code that is then run on contributors' computers. Or not. If code doesn't run, or generates errors, the problems can be readily identified and the code either rejected or repaired by the contributor or other interested members of the community. The advent of email, by making all members with Internet access universally available and connectable, reduced the cost of coordination and collaboration within OSS communities. Going forward, any individual with sufficient background, training, or experience in computer science could participate at little to no cost to themselves or to the community.

Threadless leverages the ubiquity of computers, graphic design software, and the Internet to transform a material good (that is, a T-shirt) into an information good. Submissions created by contributors on their own computers using their preferred graphics packages are uploaded to Threadless's website, critiqued and evaluated, and possibly reworked. Community participation takes the form of representing ideas, inspiration, and tastes as information signals that can be easily aggregated and evaluated. Threadless and the members of its community effectively share the material costs of near universal, virtual participation. Threadless developed and hosts the website

---

10 See von Hippel and Katz (2002) for a discussion on how most users may be able to innovate through manufactured supplied toolkits.

that provides the information infrastructure and platform that support and facilitate participation, and community members use their computers and design software to participate and interact with one another. In the case of InnoCentive, the tools required for participation vary with the type of problem posted. Problems for which a "paper solution," that is, a research proposal solution, is required are essentially information problems for which recourse to local knowledge stores and scientific journals is often sufficient. Problems that require a "reduction to practice" solution, that is, submission of a chemical or biological agent, are likely to attract solvers who have easy and ready access to the necessary materials and equipment. One winning solver, for example, was a retiree with a fully equipped, home-based organic chemistry laboratory that he used for his hobbies.

More generally, two trends are making the tools needed for scientific problem solving more accessible. First, much scientific work can now be done in-silico, that is, the information component of material objects is extracted and modeled and further developed on computers. Computer simulations that provide good first approximations of the viability of proposed solutions, by shrinking the solution space, reduce or eliminate the costly trial-and-error phase of bench-based problem solving. Second, the cost of physical tools needed to generate solutions is also declining rapidly and dramatically. For example, polymerase chain reaction machines used for genomic amplification and sequencing can now be purchased on eBay for less than US$1,000. InnoCentive' distributed problem solving leverages the sunk costs across the tools owned by solvers.

Distributed innovation systems are organized so as to lower the cost of participation for contributors. Reducing or eliminating barriers to entry expands the population that can self-select into the community. There typically being no screening, joining a community tends to be easy, even trivial. Neither is there any *a priori* guarantee of acceptance, which is usually earned on the basis of experience and knowledge as manifested in whatever contributions are made. With task granularity, too, the degree to which an innovation outcome depends on the contribution of any given individual is reduced. Granules of activity can be parceled out to individuals working independently, and then aggregated by those same individuals, working collaboratively, into a larger outcome. Co-creation not only limits the cost to individuals, but also, because a broader base of knowledge and perspectives is brought to bear in the creation process, tends to produce more robust innovations.

Openness and Intellectual Property

Inviting "outsiders" to participate in the innovation process naturally implies a different orientation towards issues of openness and intellectual property (IP). The traditional road to innovation, which is paved in secrecy and walled off to competitors and customers and emphasizes the accumulation of a large IP portfolio, would clearly not be effective in a distributed innovation setting in which participation is invited from many individuals. In such settings, individuals and especially organizations must be comfortable with the requisite degree of openness in the innovation process and adjust IP policies to encourage greater sharing and reuse of knowledge and expertise. There is no standard approach to evolving towards open innovation. The degree to which openness and creativity can be accommodated by IP is dependent on the context of operation and norms of the industrial setting and business model.

OSS communities represent the radical edge of openness and sharing observed to date in complex technology development. OSS communities are open in the sense that their outputs can be used by anyone (within the limits of the license), and anyone can join by subscribing to the development email list. Openness in joining leads, in turn, to transparency in the development process, since the bulk of communication about projects and their direction generally occurs in public. This means that project leadership is accountable to the wider community for growth and future direction, and also that everyone will be aware of shortfalls and issues. Transparency also affords individuals self-determination with respect to the level of effort they choose to commit, and awareness of others' efforts that they might be able to fold into their own contributions. Traditional means of IP protection (for example, copyrights and patents) are not available within the context of OSS projects. Submitted code, although nominally copyrighted to the contributors or their employers, is, according to the terms of most OSS licensing arrangements, immediately available for use and further modification by others. This ethos of sharing and modification extends beyond code to the actual technology development process in the sense that community members engage in joint problem solving via open sharing of ideas and ongoing interaction. OSS communities license code to ensure that all contributed software is available to all users both within and outside the community. Formal licensing arrangements vary greatly by project, but mostly follow the example of the Free Software Foundation in using the General Public License (GPL), which stipulates that all modifications to the source code must be made public if the modified code has been redistributed. Linux, for example, is licensed by Torvalds under the GPL, and all modifications to it by commercial entities, such as TiVo's modification to the Linux kernel for its consumer DVR, are public. Projects that do not impose this stipulation often use a Berkeley Software Distribution (BSD)-like license, which permits redistribution without release of modifications. Communities that use a BSD license, the Apache Software Foundation for example, rely on the speed of the development process and frequency of updates to ensure that all modifications come back to the community. Designers for Threadless need to feel comfortable revealing their designs to community members and accepting feedback, negative as well as positive. There is also the risk of submitted ideas inspiring others to create related but different designs that might outperform the designs that inspired them. Most designers will also need to be psychologically prepared to lose in public, as very few designs are produced. Finally, whereas non-winning designers retain all rights to their work, winning designers, in exchange for the cash prize, assign the copyright for their work, and exclusive use of the design on T-shirts, to Threadless. That Threadless management has embraced openness and transparency is reflected in most decisions about the interaction platform, voting and selection rules, and even manufacturing strategy being taken openly and in consultation with the community, which has on many occasions provided direction and guidance unanticipated by Threadless management. Recently, for example, issues of copyright infringement over a winning design were identified and rectified through direct involvement of the community. Threadless retains sufficient rights to IP to ensure the viability of its business model, but leaves rights to all other uses to the designers. The company's claims on IP are thus not based on the use of its platform.

The sine qua non of InnoCentive is the willing broadcast by seeker firms of their R&D laboratories' current difficult to solve in-house science problems, traditionally regarded as highly proprietary and often jealously guarded. InnoCentive works with firms to generalize their problems such that no company specific information is revealed. That seekers and solvers remain anonymous to one another throughout the process further mitigates the risk of releasing proprietary knowledge about internal scientific programs. A firm that finds a suitable solution to its broadcasted problem acquires the IP from the solver in exchange for the agreed prize. Most IP transfer clauses grant the seeker rights to internal use and the solver rights to use in applications not required by the seeker. Through contractual arrangements that provide for R&D unit laboratory output audits, InnoCentive ensures that solutions viewed but not acquired by seeker firms do not somehow show up in the firm's IP portfolio, thereby protecting non-winning solvers.

Currently, due to seeker firms' concerns about "clean" IP transfer and the allocation of prize money, InnoCentive solvers cannot work together or discover through other scientists on the platform complementary approaches to solving a particular problem. This naturally limits the innovative capability of the distributed network. As has been observed in OSS settings, the free flow of ideas facilitates creative solutions to often intractable problems. The limitations are not necessarily within the InnoCentive web platform; rather, it is that seeker firm's IP lawyers and managers need to become comfortable with acquiring IP created by multiple and disparate collaborators. In general, distributed innovation systems thrive when organizers embrace openness, transparency, and IP regimes that sustain continued collaborative participation.

Limitations and Extensions

Although we have presented a fairly positive view of the success and possibilities of distributed innovation systems, they are not without limitations. First, we observe a relatively high failure rate at various levels of analysis. The Linux operating system, Apache web server, and Firefox web browser are spectacularly successful and thriving, but thousands of OSS projects are stillborn. In SourceForge.net, an online repository of OSS projects, there are in excess of 100,000 software projects engaging more than 1.4 million users, but few are making any meaningful progress towards code shipment and the cultivation of active development communities.[11] At the micro-level, data from Threadless and InnoCentive reveal that most attempts to create designs and solve science problems fail. The six to 10 new T-shirt designs Threadless releases each week are selected from a base of approximately 800 new designs submitted weekly. Similarly, InnoCentive's problem resolution rate of 30 per cent is on the base of about one successful solution out of 10 submitted for each problem.

Second, there is a non-deterministic element of distributed innovation systems in that they cannot be used in the manner of traditional R&D organizations to deliver innovations "on demand" and according to annual plan. Anyone who expects strict planning guidelines and milestone-based innovation development in OSS communities will be disappointed. Contributors to these communities are not employees and they cannot be expected, nor do they care, to be in tune with the pressures and methods of sponsoring organizations. One

---

11 On an absolute basis, however, even if only 10 percent are successful, this represents more than 10,000 projects.

who desires that a particular feature be added to OSS software is well advised to develop it oneself.

Finally, there is within traditional organizations a great deal of internal resistance to embracing distributed innovation systems. Many organizations are quite good at absorbing external knowledge for internal consumption, but many fewer are comfortable being transparent about internal issues and problems that need to be resolved. Concerns about trade secrecy and IP protection are immediately raised when the distributed innovation alternative is considered. Staff often believe that revealing knowledge about internal developments will put the organization at risk and might tip off competitors about future plans. Many insiders also believe that they have a monopoly on relevant knowledge and are already in contact with knowledgeable external experts, rendering a waste of time interaction with random individuals outside the organization. A stronger but generally unstated reservation is fear of loss of employment. Some internal staff view the creation of a distributed innovation system as a first step towards outsourcing their jobs. Internal staff who are cynical about management's motives in embracing distributed innovation will resist cooperating with such efforts.

These limitations notwithstanding, many individuals and organizations have been inspired by the success of distributed innovation systems and are applying the principles to other domains. Perhaps the most successful and widely known is Wikipedia, the free online encyclopedia established in 2001. Open in this case means that virtually anyone can contribute a new article or edit an existing one. By the end of June 2006, Wikipedia had accumulated 4.2 million articles totaling 1.4 billion words in 250 languages, 2.3 million photographs and illustrations, more than five million links to other websites, and 85.4 million between-article cross-reference links, and occupied approximately 12 gigabytes. Wikipedia's explosive growth has been fueled by more than 300,000 volunteer contributors each of whom has made at least 10 changes to the encyclopedia, and two full-time system administrator employees of the non-profit Wikimedia foundation. Analysis of the quality of articles has found error rates to be only slightly higher for Wikipedia than for *Encyclopedia Britannica*.[12]

Distributed innovation systems will take hold first in areas of endeavor dominated by information and knowledge, but not necessarily limited to the purveyance of pure information goods. As more and more work of all types is done in-silico, more areas of economic activity will become amenable to

---

12 See Giles (2005) for a comparison of science articles in Wikipedia and *Encyclopedia Britannica*.

the distributed innovation model. Separation of the information and physical components of goods will likely give rise to new organizational forms that specialize in either the information or physical foundry side of production. This has occurred already in the area of application specific integrated circuits, with the design component distributed to users around the world via specialized toolkits for innovation and the manufacturing component limited to specialized silicon fabs (von Hippel 2005). A similar trend has been observed in the sports equipment industry in which manufacturers have become conduits for transforming innovations conceived by a distributed base of users into mass-market products.[13] Organizers of distributed innovation systems will be concerned not only with providing access to tools that enable information-based innovation, but also with the "architecture of participation" for contributors, which of necessity includes consideration of the intellectual property regime that underlies their efforts. The architecture of participation is concerned with designing modularity and granularity into the task structure so as to minimize the cost of, and motivate with intrinsic or extrinsic (or both) rewards, participation by contributors. The task structure should facilitate accretion of effort in a way that improves the overall quality of a desired innovation. Attempts that enable many to participate, but limit the benefits of the outcome to a few, will likely fail. Successful, sustainable efforts will be built on IP regimes that reward participation with perpetual free use, attribution of effort, direct compensation, business models that do not restrict community engagement and development, or most likely some combination of these incentives.

Conclusion

Joy's Law applies to most organizations that are responsible for continually delivering innovations to stakeholders. Distributed innovation systems are an alternative approach to organizing for innovation that seems to meet the challenge of accessing distributed knowledge. They demonstrate the effectiveness of new methods and organizational structures for improving innovation outcomes by engaging a broader base of outside knowledge holders. Traditional organizations should not, however, seize on distributed innovation systems as some silver bullet that will solve their internal innovation problems. Rather, these systems are an important addition to an organization's portfolio of innovation strategies. Those who would adopt or create a distributed

---

13 See Hienerth et al. (2006) for an economic model and case study of user driven entrepreneurial effects.

innovation system, however, must be prepared to acknowledge the locus of innovation to be outside the boundaries of the focal organization. And this will require a fundamental reorientation of views about incentives, task structure, management, and intellectual property.

References

Amor-Iglesias, J.J. et al. (2005) Measuring Libre Software Using Debian 3.1 (Sarge) as A Case Study: Preliminary Results, *Upgrade* (6:3), 13–16.

Baldwin, C.Y. and Clark, K.B. (2006) The Architecture of Participation: Does Code Architecture Mitigate Free Riding in the Open Source, *Management Science* (52:7), 1116–27.

Baldwin, C.Y., Hienerth, C. and von Hippel, E. (2006) How User Innovations Become Commercial Products: a Theoretical Investigation and Case Study, *Research Policy* (35:9), 1291–313.

Csikszentmihalyi, M. (1990) *Flow: The Psychology of Optimal Experience*, New York, Harper and Row.

Giles, J. (2005) Internet Encyclopedias go Head to Head, *Nature* (438:15), 900–901.

Hayek, F. (1945) The Use of Knowledge in Society, *The American Economic Review* (35:4), 519, 530.

von Hippel (1994) 'Sticky Information' and the Locus of Problem Solving: Implications for Innovation, *Management Science* (40:4), 429–39.

von Hippel, E. (2005) *Democratizing Innovation*, Cambridge, MA: MIT Press.

von Hippel, E. and Katz, R. (2002) Shifting Innovation to Users via Toolkits, *Management Science* (48:7), 821–33.

Lakhani, K. and Wolf, R. (2005) Why Hackers Do What They Do: Understanding Motivation and Effort in Free/Open Source Software Projects. In Feller, J., Fitzgerald, B. and Hissam, S. (eds), *Perspectives on Free and Open Source Software*. Cambridge: MIT Press.

Riggs, W. and von Hippel, E. (1994) Incentives to Innovate and the Sources of Innovation: The Case of Scientific Instruments, *Research Policy*.

2

Firms' Participation
in Free/Open Source Projects:
Theory and Preliminary Evidence

Andrea Bonaccorsi, Dario Lorenzi, Monica Merito and Cristina Rossi

1. Introduction

It has been widely acknowledged that the projects of the free and open source software (FOSS) community represent an impressive example of successful collective action processes (von Hippel and von Krogh, 2003). Indeed, thousands of developers, who do not receive any direct monetary compensation and work in a decentralised manner, have succeeded in providing an enormous amount of code, often supplying high-quality and complex programs (Benussi, 2006). Even more surprisingly, the movement has evolved considerably in recent years and OSS has gained an increasing economic importance. Despite the dominance of proprietary standards, more and more users are now running FOSS programs on their systems (Ghosh, 2006), while new agents are taking part in the collective action by adopting open standards or using them in their productive processes. They are public bodies, universities and research centres, and even for-profit firms, which witness how the idea, proposed by the Open Source Initiative[1] in 1998, of getting the open source world closer to the commercial one, has been extremely farsighted. Several empirical analyses have shown that more and more software firms, including also several large market incumbents,[2] are now involved, to various extents, in the movement (Bonaccorsi et al., 2006). In this framework, this chapter focuses on the relationships between these companies

---

1 http://www.opensource.org.
2 Think for instance of IBM, which has been involved in Linux development since 1998.

and the open source community; namely, the issue of firms' involvement in the FOSS projects is addressed.

At present, there is plenty of evidence that open projects are much more than anarchical communities joined only by ideologically oriented individuals writing code in their spare time on a voluntary basis.[3] However, up to now, most studies on the relationships between commercial firms and the free/open source movement have tended to focus either on ways of doing business out of open standards (Kosky, 2005), or on the motivations of companies to take part in these projects (Rossi and Bonaccorsi, 2006; Bitzer, 2004). These studies reveal that firms exploit the code base provided by the FOSS community as a basis for preparing software solutions to offer to their customers. Few studies (see for instance Henkel, 2006) have investigated whether and how these companies directly feed, in their turn, such code base by contributing their own developments back to the open projects.

Moreover, under a methodological viewpoint, it is worth noting that most of these analyses have been carried out through case studies or by gathering survey data.

Thus, the contribution of this chapter to the literature is in investigating whether and how firms contribute to the projects of the FOSS community, using a methodology based on the analysis of the projects hosted on the largest FOSS repository, SourceForge.[4]

We aim at providing original empirical evidence on three main research questions: (i) Do profit firms act not only as *takers* but also as *givers* by directly contributing to FOSS projects hosted on SourceForge? (ii) If yes, what do firms do within the projects? Do they only carry out ancillary works (bug fixing, mailing list assistance, etc.) or do they also provide code and undertake coordination activities? Moreover, (iii) does the presence of firms shape the evolution of these projects? Namely, are there significant differences between projects participated in by firms and the others? Finally, based on the empirical findings, a research agenda for future developments is provided.

---

3   It is worth noting that the romantic idea of a 13-year-old smart programmer writing open code during the night is a myth of the Open Source that needs to be put into perspective. Several authors have shown through empirical research (see for instance Hertel et al., 2003, Hars and Ou, 2002) the massive presence of people working in the IT sector among the FOSS developers' communities. Dahlander and McKelvey (2005) confirm these results, acknowledging the presence of developers with a degree in software engineering.

4   http://www.sourceforge.net.

The chapter is organised as follows: section 2 surveys the literature on firms' involvement in the FOSS movement; section 3 describes data and methodology; section 4 summarises the results of the empirical investigation; section 5 concludes and discusses the research agenda.

2. Firms' Participation in the Free/Open Source Movement: a Review of the Literature

An increasing body of literature investigates the changes occurring within the free/open source movement in recent years. From a social phenomenon with a strong ideological connotation (Raymond, 2000), it is now evolving to an economic reality deeply affecting industrial dynamics within the software industry (Gehring, 2006).

Particularly, commercial firms take part in the FOSS movement in different ways. Historically, the first form of involvement has been the gifting of code by large software companies to the open source community, as in the well known case of Netscape, which in 1998 released its Navigator under a FOSS licence, giving rise to the Mozilla project. Other incumbents of the software market followed its example (Wichmann, 2002) and, nowadays, even Microsoft is opening to FOSS by turning over several of its programs to FOSS developers, playing a role in a process that the company has strongly criticised in the past.

However, it is not only a matter of business strategy for large software companies. At present, the phenomenon of software companies' engagement in FOSS activities is becoming fairly widespread. More and more firms are entering the market by using open code downloaded from the Internet as an input for providing to their customers open source-based products and services. Bonaccorsi et al. (2006) have extensively described the phenomenon, calling these agents *open source firms*.[5] Using data from a large-scale survey on 146 Italian open source firms, we found a wide diffusion of *hybrid business models* that mix the offering of open solutions with the provision of proprietary software. In the same survey, almost half of the respondents claimed to participate (or to have participated) actively in the projects of the FOSS community (Bonaccorsi and Rossi, 2003) and the results were confirmed by another survey we carried out on a European context.[6]

---

5   On the contrary, proprietary firms are the ones that entirely base their activity on proprietary programs.

6   The survey was conducted in five countries (Finland, Germany, Italy, Portugal and Spain).

The issue of firms' contributions to the FOSS community is intriguing from an economic viewpoint. It is a case of participation in collective action by profit companies for which it is hard to advocate the intrinsic and extrinsic motivations[7] commonly cited to explain individual engagement in the private provision of collective goods (Elster, 1985, 1998). Specifically, in terms of developers' participation in FOSS projects, the literature has acknowledged the importance of motivations related to having fun programming (Luthiger and Jungwirth, 2007; Torvalds and Diamonds, 2001), embracing the values of the FOSS movement and signalling talent in the hope of being hired by large software firms (Lerner and Tirole, 2002).

However, firms' participation in collective actions has been poorly investigated by economic scholars.[8] To the best of our knowledge, the studies that have explored how firms contribute to the code base provided by the FOSS community have focused on a single project or on a limited number of firms, often using case studies or other qualitative methodologies. For example, Henkel (2006) focusing on companies' participation in the development of embedded Linux, has provided evidence that firms do selectively reveal their code, even if in different ways and proportions, depending on their characteristics. Several studies have highlighted how firms benefit from FOSS participation. Some authors (Dahlander and Wallin, 2006; Dahlander and Magnusson, 2005; Lin, 2006) have shown that companies involved in the movement are surrounded by an open environment in which they benefit from external sources of innovation outside their boundaries. Watson et al. (2005) have referred to *transaction benefits* (as opposed to *transaction costs*) stemming from the interaction with FOSS communities. Pitt et al. (2006) have analysed the impact of the choice of FOSS-oriented strategies on a company's brand, showing that it represents a final phase in the evolution of corporate brands from closed to open brands.

Even the survey data collected by Bonaccorsi and Rossi (2003) present several shortcomings. First, they do not provide any information on the projects in which respondents take part, making difficult any characterisation of the collective action processes in which firms are involved. Second, although the

---

7   Psychological literature on these themes (Ryan and Deci, 2000) have distinguished between *extrinsic* and *intrinsic* incentives; while the former refer to the direct or indirect monetary compensation stemming from carrying on a given activity, the latter point to the *per se* satisfaction in carrying on the activity itself and have been usually invoked to explain individual participation in collective action.

8   Several works have explored firms' lobbying processes for gaining trade protection. Such processes benefit not only those firms that lobby for protection and bore the costs, but also the free riders (Olson, 2004).

authors have distinguished between coordination and simple participation, it would be interesting to know more about firms' activity within the projects and their evolution over time. Finally, it emerged from phone follow up in our study that sometimes, even the concept of participation in free/open source is surrounded by confusion, making data prone to under- and over-estimation problems.

Firms' engagement in FOSS projects represents, consequently, an opportunity to address this research gap.

3. Data and Methodology

The methodology proposed in this chapter aims at addressing the issue of commercial firms' participation in FOSS projects by collecting data from SourceForge, currently the largest open source repository[9] available on the Internet. The data-gathering procedure helps overcome some of the shortcomings highlighted in the previous section. Indeed, SourceForge provides plenty of information about the hosted projects, while the collection of information through the repository (and other related websites) eliminates the risk of subjective interpretation of the questions to which survey data are prone.

We sampled 300 projects out of 140,000 currently hosted on the repository, selected on the basis of their level of activity. SourceForge provides detailed criteria for assessing the level of activity of a project. Such criteria are based on several metrics, such as the intensity of use of the instruments offered by the repository (e.g. forums, mailing lists); the bug-reporting activity; the number of downloads or web pages visits per day, etc. On these bases, the repository provides a classification of the hosted projects: we selected the 300 projects ranking at the top positions. It is worth noting that a similar sampling procedure has been widely used in the literature (see for instance Klincewicz, 2005). The selection of sample projects among active ones depends on the period in which data gathering has been undertaken. Indeed, the position of a project in the rank changes every day, the fact that the project has not been abandoned being the only constant thing. Indeed, the current active state of the project is the most important element we wish to take into account in our research, so that we investigate a snapshot of the evolution of the FOSS movement at the moment of the survey. However, we are aware that some sampling biases may exist as we

---

9   As of today, the repository hosts 260,000 projects and 2.7 million users.

expect that the most active projects have the greatest chance of showing firm involvement.

The repository itself was an important source of information. Indeed, for each project, SourceForge provides detailed information on: number of developers and administrators; date of registration on the repository; type of licence under which the code is released; intended audience (e.g. advanced users vs. end users); typology of products (e.g. Internet software vs. management software); compatibility with different operating systems; the use of mailing lists and forums; the bug-reporting activities, etc. (e.g. the programming languages or the availability of translations into foreign languages).

Nevertheless, it was not possible to detect firms involved by using only the repository. Data on companies' participation have been collected mainly through projects' websites and other instruments outside SourceForge, in particular mailing lists and forums.

In short, the constructed database contains the variables shown in Table 2.1.

Table 2.1 The variables in the database

Variables
Number of developers
Number of administrators
Type of licence
Bugs
Date of registration
Number of mailing lists
Number of messages in public forums
Compatibility with Linux
Compatibility with Windows
Compatibility with other open source systems
Awards won
Programming languages
Typology of products
Intended audience
Number of donators
Type of database
Development phase

Table 2.1   *Concluded*

Variables
Translations into foreign languages
Support requests
Patches
Feature requests
Elements in subversion
Downloads daily
Visited web pages inside SourceForge daily
Presence of firms
Type of firms' involvement

4. Main Results

The most important characteristics of the 300 sampled projects are summarised below.

Project dimensions. In line with previous studies on the topic (see for instance Ghosh et al., 2002a, 2002b), we find the developing team to be fairly narrow: the median number of programmers is seven, while 15.0 per cent of the projects have only one participant.[10]

Licences. As expected (Lerner and Tirole, 2005), the most widespread licence is GNU General Public Licence (GNU GPL, 57.9 per cent), followed by its derivation (LGPL, with 12.8 per cent), by BSD licence (7.8 per cent), Mozilla Public Licence 1.1 (5.4 per cent), and Apache Licence 2.0 (3.9 per cent).

Technical aspects. The instruments that the repository puts at the disposal of developers have revealed to be very important for the software production process. They are widely used: almost every project has a forum; 66.0 per cent of them have at least one mailing list and over 50.0 per cent have a website hosted on SourceForge. The most widespread programming language is Java (30.0 per cent), even if the entire C family[11] is still predominant (57.0 per cent). In 74 cases out of 300 (24.7

---

10   On average, each project includes 14 developers and three coordinators.
11   For instance C, C++, visual C++, etc.

per cent), a specific database is used in the development process: MySQL has confirmed to be the most used one (47.3 per cent), followed by PostgreSQL and JDBC. Notwithstanding that the majority of the projects are released under the flagship of the FOSS licences, 55.7 per cent of the programs are compatible with Windows operating systems and 16.7 per cent are developed exclusively for these ones. These results seem a further signal of the evolution of the FOSS movement from its strong ideological origins.

Intended audience and products. Projects target mainly developers (26.9 per cent) and end users (29.2 per cent). In general, it seems that the average user has high computer science skills: 30.0 per cent of projects are clearly directed to firms, 10.0 per cent target system administrators and 4.0 per cent are devoted to advanced end users. Solutions provided by the projects are fairly heterogeneous; many different classes of products (177) have been identified: the most frequent ones are development software (26 cases, 8.7 per cent) and Internet-related applications (20 cases, 6.7 per cent).

The most relevant results are summarised in Table 2.2.

Regarding firms' participation, 97 projects out of the 300 (32.3 per cent) count the involvement of one or more firms. This result is fairly intriguing but is in line with recent developments in the economic literature which have emphasised the increasing importance of firms in the free/open source scenario. But a deeper investigation of the phenomenon is necessary to understand the evolution of the FOSS movement and its impact on the industrial dynamics of the software industry.

Companies' participation takes various forms, and it is possible to single out three main different types of involvement:

1. *project coordination* (one or more firms leading the project and organising development phases), which is the most frequent way of companies' participation, with 60 cases;

2. *collaboration* to code development, in different phases and at different extents (bug fixing, testing or offering services as distribution and assistance, writing documentation, etc: 37 cases);

3.   *provision of code* or protocols[12] (in seven cases), which means releasing part of the internally produced code to the FOSS community.

It is worth noting that the sum is 104 instead of 97, as in seven cases there is more than one firm involved in different ways in the same project (in six of these cases, there is a firm coordinating the project and one or more firms collaborating in it).

Table 2.2   Descriptive analysis of the entire sample

PROJECT DIMENSION:	
Median number of core developers	7
Percentage of projects with only one core developer	15.0%
PERCENTAGE OF PROJECTS RELEASED WITH:	
GNU General Public Licence	57.9%
LGPL	12.8%
BSD licence	7.8%
Mozilla Public Licence	5.4%
Apache Licence	3.9%
PROGRAMMING LANGUAGES: PERCENTAGES OF PROJECTS	
Written in Java	30.0%
Written in a generic C language (e.g. C, C++)	57.0%
COMPATIBILITY WITH OPERATING SYSTEMS: PERCENTAGE OF PROJECTS	
Compatible with Windows operating systems	55.7%
Developed exclusively for Windows operating systems	16.7%
TARGETED AUDIENCE: PERCENTAGE OF PROJECTS INTENDED FOR*	
Developers	26.9%
End users	29.2%
Firms	30.0%
System administrators	10.0%
Advanced end users	4.0%

* Exclusively or not.

---

12 For example, communication protocols used to share information among different devices.

The numerous cases of companies appointed as project coordinators highlight the good relationship between firms and the free/open source community. Indeed, FOSS projects have a decentralised structure and the leadership emerges from the bottom up (O'Mahony, 2003), being the consequence of the very foundation of the project, the provision of valuable code or of bright solutions to critical technical problems (Bonaccorsi et al., 2006). We investigate ways in which firms succeeded in achieving leadership in OSS (see Table 2.3). In most cases, the firm itself founded the project, but there is also evidence of companies that entered an existing project and replaced the coordinator. Seven coordinating firms were settled up by the members of the initial project group.

Table 2.3   Ways in which coordination is achieved by firms

Ways in which coordination is achieved	N	per cent
Setting up the project	36	60.0
Entrance in the project and replacement of the previous coordinators	17	28.3
The project coordination team sets up a firm	7	11.7
TOTAL	60	100.0

After analysing the role played by firms in the FOSS community, we explored whether and how their presence shapes the evolution of these projects. Several differences have been singled out between projects with and without firm participation (group A) and the others (group B). Table 2.4 summarises the results of the inferential procedures carried on to detect statistically significant differences.

In general, projects participated in by firms are larger: they are joined by more developers and have more coordinators than the others. Moreover, data seem to highlight that they show a higher level of activity, as witnessed, for instance, by the more intense bug-reporting activity and by the wider use of mailing lists. This evidence does not seem unexpected, as firms are likely to attract developers more easily and to have their own employees working on the project.

Table 2.4   Comparison between projects with or without firm participation

Characteristics of the projects	Projects with firm participation (A)	Projects with no firm participation (B)	Statistical tests performed	Lowest P value
PARTICIPATION				
Average number of developers	19	5	a, b, c, e	0.01
Average number of project coordinators	11	1	a, b, c, e	0.01
TECHNICAL ASPECTS				
Average number of mailing lists	2.61	1.69	a, b, c, e	0.01
Bug reporting activity	744	358	a, b, c, e	0.01
Future requests	222	144	a, b, c, e	0.01
Elements in SVN	605	391	a, b, c, e	0.01
Patches	189	60	a, b, c, e	0.01
Programming language: C family	40.2%	65.0%	d, e	0.05
Programming language: Java	47.4%	21.7%	d, e	0.05
Number of translations into different languages	9	5	a, b, c, e	0.01
LICENCE				
Usage of the GNU General Public	45.4%	73.9%	d, e	0.05
USERS AND PRODUCTS				
Intended audience	(1st) Developers, (2nd) end users	(1st) End users, (2nd) developers	d, e	0.05
Companies as targeted users	39.9%	12.4%	d, e	0.05

Note: Hartley's Test (a), t Test (b), Mann-Whitney U Test (c), Chi-Square Test (d) and Pearson Correlation Coefficient (e); the last column of the table reports the lowest P value obtained by all the statistical tests performed on each variable.

As expected, firms' presence has an impact on the management of intellectual property rights (IPRs). The use of the General Public Licence (GPL) is less common in projects joined by firms: the percentage of GPLed solutions decreases from 73.9 per cent in group B to 45.4 per cent in group A. It is worth noting that GPL remains, in both cases, the most appreciated alternative. These findings can be easily explained by the fact that in recent years, firms have developed their own open source licences to best suit their needs. Indeed, companies' strategies are not often accomplished by general licences as the

GPL, which also brings important limits to future decisions on licence choices, given its copyleft property.

Commercial companies also seem to shape the typology of software provided: products targeted to companies are more diffused in group A and, in general, there is evidence that the average user of the software produced within a project with firms' participation has higher computer science skills. Other technical differences deal with the use of different programming languages, with a wider presence of the Java language.

5. Conclusions and Further Developments

The empirical results reported in this work reveal that, at present, the FOSS movement differs considerably from its origins. In line with the most recent literature, the increasing role of for-profit firms is acknowledged: in almost one third of the 300 sampled projects there is some form of firms' participation. Different types of links exist between these companies and the FOSS community. Namely, firms may coordinate a project (the most frequent case), offer code or protocols, or provide other kinds of contribution in different phases of the software production process.

As expected, firms have an impact on the evolution of the projects in which they take part. Our preliminary investigations have highlighted several statistically significant differences between the projects with firm participation and the others. It has emerged that the former are larger and more active, make less use of the GPL licences, show several technical peculiarities and, in general, produce software solutions targeted mainly at companies and high-skill users.

Summing up, notwithstanding that our findings do not allow us to come to definite conclusions, they call for the definition of a clear research agenda.

First, a wider survey of literature on firms' participation in collective action is needed to disentangle the main aspects of the topic and further investigate firms' engagement in open source activities.

Second, clear research questions should drive the empirical analyses, for example:

1. Are projects in which firms are involved more successful than the others? Hence, do companies contribute crucially to the achievement of the open source software, as the founders of the Open Source Initiative[13] hoped? This is a fairly intriguing issue that poses methodological problems, as the very concept of project success is hard to define (Raja and Tretter, 2006) and requires the integration of several metrics of project activity. Moreover, some endogeneity concerns are likely to emerge. Namely, is it firms' involvement which determines the success of a project or, on the contrary, do successful projects tend to attract companies? Clearly, inferential procedures, which we have used up to now, are not suitable for addressing these issues: the definition of empirical models and the application of appropriate econometric techniques are required.

2. What are the characteristics of the firms involved in FOSS projects? Up to now, we have explored the topic through case studies, which focused on the relationships between companies and projects. However, data should be gathered on structural characteristics of these firms (e.g. size, age, competences, product/service portfolio, etc.) in order to inquire whether and how they differ from those following a traditional software production process and how these differences are related to project participation.

3. Moreover, a wide literature (Chesbrough et al., 2006) is now exploring the so-called *open innovation model*, according to which firms can achieve a greater return on their innovative activities by using a broad range of sources (Chesbrough, 2003). Open source is a clear example of an open innovation approach (West and Gallagher, 2006). On one hand, the FOSS community is a large knowledge base from which firms can get information, and on the other side, FOSS licences are designed to foster instead of prevent access to information. In this framework, it is then of interest to explore how project participation shapes the innovation activity of the involved firms. In short, are these firms more innovative than others?

---

13 'We in the open source community have learned that this rapid evolutionary [software production] process produces better software than the traditional closed … Open Source Initiative exists to make this case to the commercial world', from the website of the Open Source Initiative, http://www.opensource.org/.

References

Bezroukov, N. (1999) Open Source Software Development as a Special Type of Academic Research (Critique of Vulgar Raymondism), *First Monday*, peer-reviewed journal on the Internet, 10(4). http://firstmonday.org/htbin/cgiwrap/bin/ojs/index.php/fm/article/view/696/606, accessed on October 18 2010.

Benussi, L. (2006) The History of the Free/Libre Open Source Software: Stories from the Open Source Evolution. In A. Bonaccorsi and C. Rossi (eds) *Economic Perspective on Open Source Software*, Franco Angeli.

Bitzer, J. (2004) Commercial Versus Open Source Software: the Role of Product Heterogeneity in Competition, *Economic Systems* 28, 369–81.

Bonaccorsi, A., Giannangeli, S. and Rossi, C. (2006) Adaptive Entry Strategies Under Competing Standards – Hybrid Business Models in the Open Source Software Industry, *Management Science*, 52(7), 1085–98.

Bonaccorsi, A. and Rossi C. (2003) *Contributing to the Common Pool Resources in Open Source Software. A Comparison Between Individuals and Firms*, SSRN Working Paper. http://papers.ssrn.com/sol3/papers.cfm?abstract_id=430920, accessed on October 18 2010.

Bonaccorsi, A. and Rossi, C. (2006) Motivations to Take Part in the Open Source Movement, *Knowledge, Technology & Policy* (Winter), 18(4), 40–64.

Chesbrough, H.W. (2003) *Open Innovation: The New Imperative for Creating and Profiting From Technology*, Harvard Business School Press.

Chesbrough, H., Vanhaverbeke, W. and West, J. (2006) *Open Innovation: Researching a New Paradigm*, Oxford University Press.

Dahlander, L. and Magnusson, M.G. (2005) Relationships Between Open Source Software Companies and Communities: Observations from Nordic Firms, *Research Policy*, 34(4), 481–93.

Dahlander, L. and McKelvey, M. (2005) Who is not Developing Open Source Software? Non-users, Users, and Developers, *Economics of Innovation and New Technology*, 14, 617–35.

Dahlander, L. and Wallin, M. (2006) A Man on the Inside: Unlocking Communities as Complementary Assets, *Research Policy*, 35(8), 1243–59.

Elster, J. (1985) Rationality, Morality, and Collective Action, *Ethics*, 96, 136–55.

Elster, J. (1998) Emotions and Economic Theory, *Journal of Economic Literature*, 36, 47–74.

Gehring, R.A. (2006) The Institutionalization of Open Source, *Poiesis Prax*, 4, 54–73.

Ghosh, R.A. (2006) Economic Impact of the Open Source Software on Innovation and Competitiveness of the Information and Communication Technologies (ICT) Sector in the EU, final report for the European Commission. http://ec.europa.eu/enterprise/sectors/ict/files/2006-11-20-flossimpact_en.pdf, last accessed October 18 2010.

Ghosh, R.A., Glott, R., Krieger, B. and Robles, G. (2002a) Survey of Developers, Free/Libre and Open Source Software: Survey and Study, *FLOSS Final Report*, International Institute of Infonomics, Berlecom Research GmbH.

Ghosh, R.A., Glott, R. and Robles, G. (2002b) Software Source Code Survey, Free/Libre and Open Source Software: Survey and Study, *FLOSS Final Report*, International Institute of Infonomics, Berlecom Research GmbH.

Ghosh, R. and Prakash, V.V. (2000) The Orbiten Free Software Survey, *First Monday*, peer-reviewed journal of the Internet, 5(7). http://firstmonday.org/htbin/cgiwrap/bin/ojs/index.php/fm/article/view/769/678, last accessed October 18 2010.

Hars, A. and Ou, S. (2002) Working for Free? Motivations for Participating in Open-Source Projects, *International Journal of Electronic Commerce*, 6, 25–39.

Henkel, J. (2006) Selective Revealing in Open Innovation Processes: The Case of Embedded Linux, *Research Policy*, 35, 953–69.

Hertel, G., Niedner, S. and Herrmann, S. (2003) Motivation of Software Developers in Open Source Projects: An Internet-based Survey of Contributors to the Linux Kernel, *Research Policy*, 32, 1159–77.

Klincewicz, K. (2005) *Innovativeness of Open Source Software Projects*, MIT Working Papers.

Kosky, H. (2005) OSS Production and Licensing Strategies of Software Firms, *Review of Economic Research on Copyright Issues*, 2(2), 111–25.

Lerner, J. and Tirole, J. (2002) Some Simple Economics of Open Source, *Journal of Industrial Economics*, 50, 197–234.

Lerner, J. and Tirole, J. (2005) The Economics of Technology Sharing: Open Source and Beyond, *Journal of Economic Perspectives*, 19(2), 99–120.

Lin, Y. (2006) Hybrid Innovation: How Do OSS Firms Collaborate With the FLOSS Community, *Knowledge, Technology and Policy*, 18(4), 86–100.

Luthiger, B. and Jungwirth, C. (2007) Pervasive Fun, *First Monday*, peer-reviewed journal on the Internet (12:1). http://firstmonday.org/htbin/cgiwrap/bin/ojs/index.php/fm/rt/printerFriendly/1422/1340. last accessed on October 18 2010.

O'Mahony, S. (2003) Guarding the Commons: How Community Managed Software Projects Protect Their Work, *Research Policy*, 32, 1179–98.

Olson, K.M. (2004) *Free Riders Among the Rent-Seekers: A Model of Firm Participation in Antidumping Petitions*, SSRN Working Paper.

Pitt, L., Watson, R.T., Berthon, P., Wynn, D. and Zinkhan, G. (2006) The Penguin's Window: Corporate Brands From an Open-Source Perspective, *Journal of the Academy of Marketing Science*, 34(2), 115–27.

Raja, U. and Tretter, M.J. (2006) *Investigating Open Source Project Success: A Data Mining Approach to Model Formulation, Validation and Testing*, SUGI 31 Proceedings. http://www2.sas.com/proceedings/sugi31/toc.html, last accessed October 18 2010.

Raymond, E. (2000) *The Cathedral and the Bazaar*, O'Reilly.

Rossi, C. and Bonaccorsi, A. (2006) Intrinsic Motivations and Profit-Oriented Firms in Open Source Software. Do Firms Practise What They Preach? In Bitzer, J. and Schroeder, P.J.H. (eds) *The Economics of Open Source Software Development Analyzing Motivation, Organization, Innovation and Competition in the Open Source Software Revolution*, Elsevier, 83–110.

Ryan, R.M. and Deci, E.L. (2000) Intrinsic and Extrinsic Motivations: Classic Definitions and New Directions, *Contemporary Educational Psychology*, 25(1), 54–67.

Torvalds, L. and Diamonds, D. (2001) *Just for Fun: The Story of an Accidental Revolutionary*, HarperBusiness.

von Hippel, E. and von Krogh, G. (2003) Open Source Software and the Private-Collective Innovation Model: Issues for Organization Science, *Organization Science*, 14(2), 209–23.

von Holzinger, K. (2003) *The Problems of Collective Action: A New Approach*, SSRN Working Paper.

Watson, R.T., Boudreau, M., Greiner, M., Wynn, D., York, P. and Gul, R. (2005) Governance and Global Communities, *Journal of International Management*, 11(2), 125–42.

West, J. and Gallagher, S. (2006) Patterns of Open Innovation in Open Source Software. In Chesbrough, H., Vanhaverbeke, W. and West, J. (eds) (2006) *Open Innovation: Researching a New Paradigm*, Oxford University Press.

Wichmann, T. (2002) *Firms' Open Source Activities: Motivations and Policy Implications*, Final Report, Free/Libre and Open Source Software (FLOSS): Survey and Study, International Institute of Infonomics, Berlecom Research GmbH.

Open Source Software in the Public Sector: Results from the Emilia-Romagna Open Source Survey (EROSS)[1]

Francesco Rentocchini[2] and Dimitri Tartari[3]

Introduction

This chapter presents the results of a study on free/libre open source software (FLOSS) adoption by public administrations (PAs) located in Emilia-Romagna. This is a well-developed Italian region that has adopted an information society plan since 1999, and is characterised by strong commitments towards e-government investments (€120 million in the period 2002–2005). It relies on a strong tradition of efficient and innovative public administrations and has collaborations with several universities present on the territory.

The results of the survey show a lively pattern inside the region, with several administrations relying on FLOSS (70 per cent of our sample). There is a significant number of organisations managing servers exclusively through FLOSS. A small number of PAs have decided to go even further and have adopted FLOSS applications at the desktop side. Finally, when the intensity

1   The authors would like to thank Sandra Lotti and Marco Mancini from the Emilia-Romagna region and the UNDERSTAND project. Moreover, the help of Angela Dimonopoli from Bocconi University and Emiliano Prampolini from CRC Emilia-Romagna is gratefully acknowledged. Finally we kindly thank Franco Sacerdotti and Fabrizio Benati of Certhidea s.r.l., together with all the PAs that took part in the survey. The opinions expressed in this work reflect those of the authors and do not necessarily reflect those of the institutions with which they are affiliated.
2   Doctoral student in law and economics, Department of Economics, University of Bologna, Italy; email: francesc.rentocchin2@unibo.it.
3   Dimitri Tartari, Italian National Centre for Informatics in Public Administrations (CNIPA) and CRC Project; email: d.tartari@crcitalia.it.

of FLOSS utilisation is compared between client and server we find FLOSS adoption follows a certain pattern. This adoption usually starts from the server side and only after it has sufficiently developed, it shifts to the client side. We conclude our analysis with pointing out advantages and disadvantages connected with FLOSS adoption by local governments.

The ICT Regional Sector: From a National to a Regional Perspective

It is well recognised that the most competitive economies all over the world are characterised by a set of common factors, i.e. the presence of a lively ICT sector together with the diffusion of ICTs all over the society (Van Ark et al., 2003). Furthermore, one of the factors contributing mostly to the productivity gap between the US and Europe is the difference in the intensity of adoption of ICT in the production of goods and services.

This means that both ICT supply and demand must be favoured by economic policies as a prerequisite for productivity growth and, as a consequence, for economic growth. To do that, the availability of ICT and the intensity of its adoption must be encouraged as the most important strategic factor, favouring both human capital investment and competitiveness.

Given the central role played by ICTs nowadays in both the economy and society, how their adoption can be increased should be investigated. PAs should cover a central role in this respect, as they can both reduce costs and increase the quality of services provided through technology adoption.

In recent years, the Emilia-Romagna regional government moved in this direction, following European guidelines. Indeed, all the projects that have been launched in the last 10 years were targeted to foster the growth of the 'knowledge economy' where the role of ICTs is paramount.

In order to spur the development of the ICT sector, Emilia-Romagna put forward a set of actions aimed at:

1. Sustaining and incentivising their adoption by both citizens and companies.

2. Guiding expenditure in ICTs by PAs and investment more generally by local municipalities.

Examples of the programmes that have been put in practice following the above-mentioned guidelines are:

1. *The regional programme for industrial research, innovation and technological transfer (PRRIITT).* Its main objective is to strengthen the regional production system by different means: (a) stimulate applied research in both competitive and innovative areas, (b) increase the innovative content in the production of goods and services and (c) stimulate the growth of the regional knowledge economy.

2. *The regional telematic plan 2002–2005.* It contains provisions to invest resources in the telecommunication infrastructure named LEPIDA (a regional broadband network owned by the regional government itself). In addition, it prescribes the creation of applicative platforms devoted to several tasks, among which it is worth mentioning the modernisation of the labour organisation and the rationalisation of internal processes to provide citizens and companies with more efficient public services.

FLOSS and Public Administrations

The free/libre open source software (FLOSS) is a phenomenon that has received an increasing importance in recent years. Its diffusion and reliability have improved at an outstanding pace both at the public and private level. Both PAs and private enterprises have implemented FOSS products and started to rely heavily on the advantages characterising this alternative method of software production (Bonaccorsi and Rossi, 2003).

PAs have notably been at the forefront of these dynamics, and the predominance of studies concerning PAs can be explained in the following three ways:

1. First, a PA is seen as an obvious place for the implementation of FLOSS. In fact, public organisations respond to a set of different incentives and have different aims to those in the private sector. Above all, they tend to provide citizens with services of high quality: FLOSS is likely to be a useful instrument for accomplishing this task. FLOSS's high technical quality and the saving on licence fees from private software vendors are factors affecting the productivity of services provided by PAs (Ghosh, 2003; Lerner and Tirole, 2002).

2.   Interesting case studies have shown that a structured adoption of FLOSS by local governments has fostered the rate of development of the relative local community. An emblematic example is surely the Extremadura region in Spain where a concerted adoption of OSS has encouraged the entrepreneurial spirit in the Extremadura ICT sector and has spurred the creation of innovative business activities.[4]

3.   The development of a bundle of high-level competences is fostered by the adoption of FLOSS. Indeed, developing tailored solutions inside public administration is a way to invest in employees' competences (Varian and Shapiro, 2003).

Many studies have dealt with the state of the art of FLOSS in PAs.[5] These studies have been mainly descriptive and the reasons behind FLOSS adoption by public bodies and its impact have been largely disregarded. To our knowledge, the only contribution in this direction is the Free/Libre Open Source Software – Policy Support (FLOSSPOLS) study. This is a government survey conducted with both local and regional government authorities in 13 European countries in 2005. The main results from this study reveal that FLOSS is used in about half of the EU local government authorities, while almost 70 per cent of FLOSS users and 38 per cent of FLOSS non-users are eager to use FLOSS in the future. This study also provides a preliminary account of both important drivers and main barriers to the adoption of FLOSS in government bodies (Glott and Ghosh, 2005).

The Emilia-Romagna government has been quite active in its use of FLOSS and has put forward two main initiatives relative to software and its applications with particular interest to FLOSS. These initiatives are the observatory for innovation and technological transfer on open source software (OITOS) and the Emilia-Romagna open source survey (EROSS).

OITOS is a newly constituted organisation mainly concentrating on FLOSS from the point of view of private enterprises. Its main objective is to provide companies with useful information about tools and standards from the ICT

---

4   For an exhaustive description of the Extremadura case study see http://ec.europa.eu/idabc/en/document/1637/470.

5   In addition to studies concerning the situation of government organisations in general, such as OSOSS (OSOSS, 2004) and FLOSSPOLS, several studies have dealt with more specific cases. An exhaustive list of European case studies is available at the Open Source Software Observatory website (see http://ec.europa.eu/idabc/en/chapter/470).

world with a particular emphasis on FLOSS. FLOSS is seen as a strategically important instrument to support both innovation and economic growth in the region.

EROSS, meanwhile, deals with PAs focusing mainly on the state-of-the-art and practices on FLOSS adoption.

The Emilia-Romagna Open Source Survey (EROSS)

The main activity of EROSS has been to create a clear picture of FLOSS usage inside the Emilia-Romagna region. In particular, we prepared a survey to investigate the intensity of adoption together with the level of penetration of FLOSS inside Emilia-Romagna municipalities.

The empirical study was conducted in collaboration with the Emilia-Romagna region and its regional competence centre for e-government and information society (CRC) and is composed of three main parts.

First, several interviews with PAs and their suppliers, both active in FLOSS adoption and distribution, were carried out. Managers of information systems from the municipalities of Modena, Argenta, Reggio Emilia and the AUSL of Parma were interviewed. The aim was to collect opinions and experiences which may help us in the difficult task of understanding factors affecting public administrations' processes together with their needs.

Second, a specific online questionnaire was submitted to all Emilia-Romagna municipalities. The questionnaire was built up keeping in mind research previously accomplished at both the national and international level. In particular, the FLOSSPOLS study played a major role in guiding us with the choice of questions and implementation procedure (Glott and Ghosh, 2005).

All the managers of information system divisions were able to access the online questionnaire and fill it in at any time. The number of collected answers was 90, which corresponds to a response rate of 26.4 per cent.

In the second stage, the aggregate of the inspected municipalities was investigated in order to check the sample's representability.

Overall, the number of software typologies which were individuated in the survey is equal to 20. We have grouped them in four main categories according to the domain of application: client/desktop, server, web and management system.

Furthermore, in order to measure both the diffusion and the pervasiveness of FLOSS adoption we built an index of utilisation intensity. This is simply equal to the number of FLOSS instalments over the total number of instalments. The construction of this index, as it will be shown in the following paragraph, is very useful for distinguishing between a marginal use of FLOSS, i.e. test or simple curiosity, and a more consistent and effective adoption.

Moreover, we created the questionnaire so that it could easily be integrated with already available data gathered by the Emilia-Romagna benchmark study UNDERSTAND (Regione Emilia-Romagna, 2003). Thus we were able to rely on a short and compact questionnaire which was very useful in obtaining a higher response rate.

Hence, the purpose of the questionnaire was threefold: evaluating the intensity of FLOSS adoption in specific areas (clients, servers, web, etc.), collecting information of both FLOSS and proprietary software, and integrating it with data from other sources, in particular with data from the project UNDERSTAND.

Results and Discussion

The first striking result, shown in Figure 3.1, points out to the presence of unaware FLOSS adopters, i.e. municipalities answering that they do not have FLOSS instalments and, at the same time, that they own some open source applications. This pattern is present in results from FLOSSPOLS as well (Glott and Ghosh, 2005). To us, this result is a hint of the small amount of knowledge available on FLOSS to Emilia-Romagna municipalities.

The percentage of FLOSS adopters inferred by EROSS 2006 survey was quite high, i.e. 70 per cent of respondents were found to have adopted FLOSS. If we compare this result with the same information obtained by UNDERSTAND we find a mismatch. Indeed, there we find a percentage of FLOSS adopters lower than 38 per cent (UNDERSTAND, 2005). FLOSSPOLS reports similar statistics to EROSS concerning the percentage of FLOSS adopters, namely almost 80 per cent over a total of 955 European local governments (Glott and Ghosh, 2005, p.17).

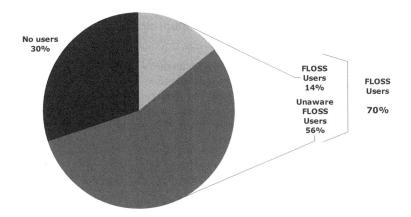

Figure 3.1   Municipalities adopting FLOSS (both aware and unaware users)

Source: EROSS (2006)

The high value of our estimate and the one from the FLOSSPOLS study must be attributed to a self-selection mechanism: users most interested in FLOSS are more likely to have answered the questionnaire we sent.

As mentioned earlier, the EROSS questionnaire has been integrated with data collected from UNDERSTAND survey. Merging the two datasets allowed us to display a clear picture of the characteristics of municipalities according to their FLOSS intensity of adoption. In Table 3.1 we first divide all the municipalities by the total intensity of FLOSS adoption (henceforth *ia*), i.e. no adoption (*ia* = 0 per cent) moderate adoption (*ia* < 20 per cent) and high adoption (*ia* > 20 per cent). In this way we are able to underline the main differences in adoption between municipalities and characterise them.

The main characteristics of the municipalities adopting intensively FLOSS are shown in column 1 of Table 3.1. Municipalities with a high intensity of FLOSS adoption have, on average, a large size; they are furnished with a broadband connection and they have adopted an e-government/ICT strategy. Furthermore, the presence of a formal ICT structure, the ability to develop software internally and, finally, ICT training for employees are all significant features. So, it looks as if the intense adoption of FLOSS discriminates between those municipalities which see ICT as an important strategic support for institutional activities and those which are not able to, or do not want to, go in this direction.

Table 3.1   Identikit of municipalities adopting FLOSS

	High intensity of adoption (*ia* > 20%)	Moderate intensity of adoption (*ia* < 20%)	No adoption (*ia* = 0%)
Average size (# inhabitants)	47.788	13.580	4.654
# Municipalities	22	40	28
Do not have a broadband connection	0%	10%	21.4%
Do have an e-government/ICT strategy	50%/50%	20%/27.5%	25%/14.3%
Do have at least one employee in the ICT division	63.6%	45%	21.4%
There is an ICT division	63.6%	42.5%	28.6%
Study and planning done internally	72.7%	35%	14.3%
Training in ICT organised since 2004	68.2%	42.5%	25%
Average interactivity of online services (2005)	46.5%	37.8%	28.6%
Licence fees per inhabitant	€1.93	€2.05	€2.33
Average number of ICT suppliers	5.1	3.4	2.1

Source: UNDERSTAND (2005); EROSS (2006).

In Table 3.2, relying on the same classification used earlier, we describe some of the difficulties related to ICTs' adoption by PAs. We note immediately that there are differences among the three groups. Municipalities with a high intensity of FLOSS adoption (column 1) rate both supplier's flexibility and interoperability of applications as the main obstacles to a correct implementation of ICTs. For the two other groups, namely moderate intensity (column 2) and no intensity (column 3), main obstacles are the low number of employees and high costs.

These differences in perceived obstacles can be interpreted as the causes that pushed some of the municipalities interviewed to experiment and sometimes to adopt FLOSS solutions.

Figure 3.2 shows the intensity of adoption of FLOSS in the area of client/desktop. Desktop systems, email clients, office automation (packages for personal productivity) and web browsing are the four sub-classifications that have been individuated in the area of client/desktop. The graph points out the fact that FLOSS desktop system is not widely adopted in the PAs of Emilia-Romagna (55 have installed Linux out of a total of 13,382). Moreover, more than 10 per cent of total instalments are found in only two municipalities.

Table 3.2   Obstacles to the introduction of ICT inside the PAs

Main obstacles to the adoption of the ICTs in public administrations (% municipalities)	High intensity of adoption (*ia* > 20%)	Moderate intensity of adoption (*ia* < 20%)	No adoption (*ia* = 0%)
Software flaws	4.55%	7.50%	17.86%
Reduced flexibility of suppliers	**36.36%**	7.50%	0.00%
Low interoperability of applications	**59.09%**	25.00%	25.00%
Low number of employees	13.64%	**30.00%**	**57.14%**
Difficulty in recruiting qualified employees	27.27%	10.00%	10.71%
Outdated ICT strategy	18.18%	20.00%	32.14%
High costs	27.27%	**57.50%**	**57.14%**
Early introduction of new versions of software	4.55%	12.50%	14.29%

Source: UNDERSTAND (2005); EROSS (2006).

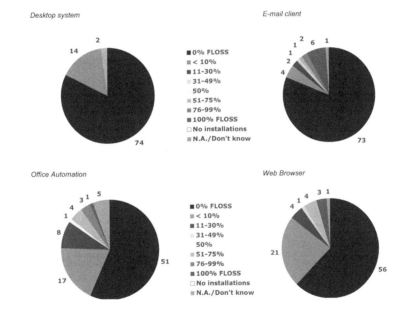

Figure 3.2   Software client/desktop (# municipalities)
Source: EROSS (2006)

On the contrary office automation, email and web browsing are all cases where the intensity of adoption of FLOSS is very high (*ia* > 50 per cent). It is worth noting that the different levels in the intensity of adoption can be interpreted as the different stages a municipality goes through a complete migration: test phase (*ia* < 30 per cent), experimentation (30 per cent < *ia* < 49 per cent) and utilisation/migration (*ia* > 50 per cent).

Overall, the number of municipalities adopting FLOSS from the client/ desktop side is not negligible. Indeed, a complete migration towards FLOSS is very complex. This is why these figures must be interpreted as very promising.

In Figure 3.3 we display the intensity of FLOSS adoption relative to web servers. It is worth noting that few municipalities have internalised web server management and, as is shown in Figure 3.4, servers in general. Nevertheless, the majority of them are using FLOSS.

Moreover, 10 municipalities manage their own servers exclusively through FLOSS. Despite this, only 44 per cent of the web servers have installed Apache. This is contrary to the world average of 60 per cent concerning Apache.[6]

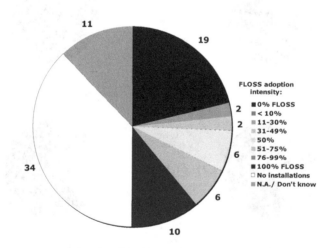

Figure 3.3   Web server (# municipalities)
Source: EROSS (2006)

---

6   For details see web server surveys at http://news.netcraft.com/ last accessed on October 18 2010.

From statistics obtained in Figure 3.4 we can see that 10 per cent of municipalities manage applications, mail and file servers exclusively via FLOSS. This points to the role that FLOSS has acquired in the last 10 years in the management of critical services such as mail servers, file servers and application servers.

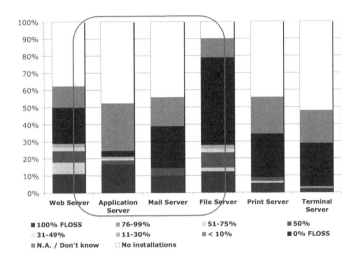

Figure 3.4   Software on the server side (percentage of municipalities)
Source: EROSS (2006)

The applications used to manage and share web content vary widely (Figure 3.5) and illustrate well the large number of existing FLOSS communities behind their development. Concerning municipalities in Emilia-Romagna, we note that there is no diffused adoption of instruments such as content management systems and groupware. Available data show that there is no clear predominance of one type of software over any other.

The answers collected on dedicated software, which is software tailored for PAs' specific needs, have been grouped in seven different functional areas: economic-financial accounting, vital statistics, administration of the personnel, attendances, protocols, financial accounting, and management of the resolutions. These areas have not shown any adoption of FLOSS. In fact, preliminary interviews conducted on selected suppliers of the PAs have pointed out the fact that the market of dedicated software is essentially ruled by a restricted number of suppliers (11 in total) with half of them being Italians and the other half

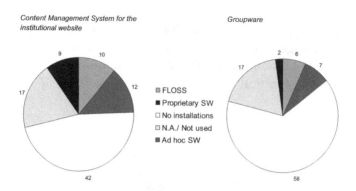

Figure 3.5   Software on the web side (# municipalities)
Source: EROSS (2006)

coming from Emilia-Romagna. This means that, pertaining dedicated software, customisation and strong ties with clients are very important. General purpose software, on the other hand, can be migrated more easily to FLOSS given the presence of lighter ties among PAs and regional companies.

In Figure 3.6, we compare the intensity of adoption of FLOSS in the area of client/desktop with the intensity on the server side. We depict single municipalities by means of bubbles of different sizes representing the number of inhabitants. From the figure we individuate a precise path of FLOSS adoption. According to this, municipalities that first start adopting FLOSS on the desktop systems (bubbles on the horizontal axis) have previously adopted it on the servers (bubbles on the vertical axis). Indeed, the number of municipalities is heavily clustered on the left side of the graph and it is distributed almost vertically. This FLOSS path of adoption, first going upward and then turning on the right, is surely the most preferred one given the minor risks municipalities are likely to face.

On the server side, few people are interested in the migration; they are usually information system administrators. On the client side, even non-expert users are concerned which means that the migration is likely to affect employees' work routines.

Finally, in Table 3.3 we present the names of FLOSS products implemented in the PAs which replied to the questionnaire. The fact that some of these are used almost exclusively by a significant number of organisations can be taken as an implicit signal of the quality and reliability of the product, making it a good candidate for prospective adoptions.

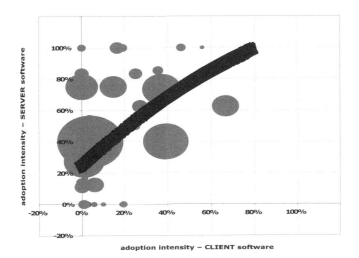

Figure 3.6   Intensity of FLOSS adoption (client/desktop vs. server)

Source: Our elaboration on EROSS (2006)

Table 3.3   Type of FLOSS adopted in Emilia-Romagna municipalities

Area of adoption	Type of FLOSS	# municipalities relying exclusively on FLOSS
Desktop/client	Linux	0
Mail	Thunderbird, Mozilla, Horde IMP, Opengroupware	6
Browser	Firefox, Mozilla, Netscape	3
Office automation	Open Office, Star Office	1
Web server	Apache	10
Application server	Tomcat, Jboss, Zope	15
Mail server	Postfix, Cyrus, Exim, Qmail, Sendmail, Squirrel	9
File server	Linux/Samba, Solaris	11
Print server	Linux/Cup	5
Terminal server	Open SSH, VNC	2
Content management system	Exo, Exponent, Ez system, FlatNuke, Joomla, Mambo, Plone	10
Groupware	E Groupware, Group Office, MoreGroupware, OpenGroupware, Plone, WebGUI	6

Source: EROSS (2006)

Conclusion

The main results obtained in the present work can be summarised as follows:

- The number of PAs adopting FLOSS, both aware and unaware, is significant (70 per cent of respondents).

- Large size, Broadband connection and the presence of e-gov/ICT strategy are all factors contributing to an intensive use of FLOSS by PAs.

- High costs and reduced number of employees are all problems for which FLOSS is seen as a solution.

- Municipalities have not taken into consideration the possibility of migrating their desktop systems to FLOSS. This type of software is perceived as closely tied to the hardware and to employees' specific competences and, for these reasons, not susceptible to immediate transfer.

- The use of applications in the area of client/desktop, personal productivity and office automation is not frequent. The main reason is the incidence of network diseconomies that makes it difficult to interact with other PAs.

- On the server side there is a number of FLOSS products which are already used by a significant number of municipalities and whose reliability make them a good choice for other PAs as well.

- The adoption of CMS and groupware is limited. The absence of a clear market leader and the availability of a high number of similar products make it difficult to select the most appropriate solution.

- Dedicated software used by the municipalities interviewed is supplied under a proprietary licence by either Italian or regional companies.

On the basis of the results obtained so far and given the need of refinement, we have been asked for a follow-up of the present analysis for the period 2007–2009. The main activities concerning the ongoing follow-up are:

- A more comprehensive dissemination of information aimed at increasing both FLOSS adoption and development by Emilia-Romagna PAs.

- A new survey to be conducted in the year 2008. In addition to PAs interviewed in the present survey we will add more public administrations previously left aside, i.e. provinces and chambers of commerce.

- Both case studies and best practices will be meticulously added. These results will be of high utility for PAs approaching FLOSS for the first time.

- A better collaboration between EROSS and OITOS in order to share the results of the two initiatives which will provide us with a clear picture of FLOSS in Emilia-Romagna from both public demand (PAs) and supply (private companies) point of view.

- Informative seminars and workshops dedicated to the PAs.

- Collaboration with European projects in order to compare our results with the ones obtained from foreign partners.

To conclude, some policy recommendations can be put forward based on the results of our study. First of all, the increase in the demand for FLOSS from Emilia-Romagna must be followed by a comparable upsurge in the supply. Indeed, it is necessary to incentivise the supply of FLOSS solutions by private companies producing software and providing services to the PAs. Furthermore, the possibility of PAs producing and distributing open source software developed internally must be taken into consideration in particular after the results of Ghosh's (2006) study. Second, the adoption of FLOSS by small PAs must be encouraged by means of investments in education and 'on-the-job' training. Finally, the high number of unaware FLOSS users points to a lack of information concerning this phenomenon. This means that appropriate diffusion of information should be done to increase adoption of FLOSS.

References

Bonaccorsi, A. and Rossi, C. (2003) Why Open Source Software Can Succeed, *Research Policy*, 32(7), 1243–58.

Ghosh, R.A. (2006) *Study on the Economic Impact of Open Source Software on Innovation and the Competitiveness of the Information and Communication Technologies (ICT) Sector in the EU*, European Commission, http://ec.europa.eu/enterprise/sectors/ict/files/2006-11-20-flossimpact_en.pdf, last accessed October 18 2010.

Ghosh, R.A. (2003) Licence Fees and GDP per Capita: The Case for Open Source in Developing Countries, *First Monday*, 12(8).

Glott, R. and Ghosh, R.A. (2005) Usage of and Attitudes towards Free/Libre and Open Source Software in European Governments: Results from the Governments Survey (FLOSSPOLS), European Commission/IST, http://www.flosspols.org/deliverables/FLOSSPOLS-D03%20local%20governments%20survey%20reportFINAL.pdf, last accessed October 18 2010.

Lerner, J. and Tirole, J. (2002) Some Simple Economics of Open Source, *Journal of Industrial Economics*, 50(2), 197–234.

OSOSS (2004) Programme for Open Standards and Open Source Software in Government (OSOSS), http://www.irisipiemonte.it/contenuti.php-include=elenco_risorse&IDcontenuto=40&lang=ita.htm, last accessed October 18 2010.

Regione Emilia-Romagna (2003) *Benchmarking della Societa dell Informazione in Emilia-Romagna*. Collana Emilia-Romagna Digitale, http://www.regionedigitale.net. last accessed October 18 2010.

Van Ark, B., Inklaar, R. and McGuckin R.H. (2003) ICT and Productivity in Europe and the United States Where Do the Differences Come From? *CESifo Economic Studies*, 49(3), 295–318.

Varian, H.R. and Shapiro, C. (2003) Linux Adoption in the Public Sector: An Economic Analysis, http://www.sims.berkeley.edu/~hal/Papers/2004/linux-adoption-in-the-public-sector.pdf. last accessed October 18, 2010.

PART II

OSS Rewards' and Incentives' Structure

The question of why so many developers dedicate time and effort into contributing to open source software projects (OSSP) without a clear return on their invested time and effort is one of the most intriguing questions in OSS research. Several studies have theorized about and empirically examined this challenging question relying on different theoretical lenses (i.e., sociology, psychology and economics) and providing a variety of reasons to explain this phenomenon. Their findings suggest that OSS communities are driven by mixed and heterogeneous motivations.

In Part II, *OSS Rewards' and Incentives' Structure*, three chapters provide different perspectives on developers' contribution to the creation of public goods.

The first chapter provides a summary of the literature on developers' motivations, suggests a research model to explain their behaviour in OSSP and provides an empirical test of the model within the context of SourceForge. net. The proposed model integrates constructs from psychology and social exchange theories to suggest several individual and social motives, how they affect developers' behaviour and some of its associated outcomes. The second chapter presents a cross-level model to explain the relationship between social capital in OSS communities and individual motivation and contribution. It discusses how community-level social capital can be created and maintained as a by-product of ongoing activities within an OSS community and illustrates some of its benefits.

Chapter 3 suggests a credit model as an alternative means to understanding the efforts developers put into the activities of OSSP. It discusses the nature of informal contracts and credits in free software, and assesses its benefits and limits.

4

What Motivates Developers in OSSP?

Hind Benbya

1. Introduction

Understanding what motivates developers to join and contribute to OSSP has received much popular and academic attention in recent years but still remains a puzzling phenomenon. Researchers investigating the subject have relied on different theoretical lenses (i.e., economics, sociology, psychology, information systems), to theorize about and explain the reasons that induce participants to join and contribute to such projects. Early studies and theorizations have largely argued that developers engage in the creation of useful and socially valuable software mainly for social and altruistic reasons (Raymond, 1999). Since then, various approaches to examining OSS developers' motives have emerged. Each of them provides several reasons for developers' participation to OSSP (e.g., Hars and Ou, 2002; Ghosh et al., 2002; Lakhani and Wolf, 2005; Shah, 2006; Benbya and Belbaly, 2010). While, our knowledge of developers' motives in OSSP is growing, understanding how developers behave in OSSP and why they behave that way, remains an open question.

This is both indicative of the relative novelty of the issue and the lack of a clear theoretical framework explaining this phenomenon. Scacchi et al. (2006) confirm this challenge and call for modeling what this process is, and how it operates, as it remains an open research question.

This chapter, therefore, aims at understanding how developers behave in OSSP, its antecedents and outcomes. For investigating this issue, we surveyed OSSP developers of SourceForge.net, the world's largest repository of OSSP, through a web-based questionnaire. The remainder of this chapter is structured as follows: we first characterize motivation studies in OSSP and describe our conceptual model (Section 2). We then describe our research methodology and data collection processes (Section 3). Next, we report our findings with respect to developers' motivation, participation levels and outcomes (Section 4). Finally, we discuss the implications of our findings (Section 5).

2. Literature Review and Main Hypotheses

The existence of several successful OSSP such as the Linux operating system, the Apache web server or even hundreds of others widely known and used applications (e.g., Mozilla, OpenOffice) or programming languages (e.g., Perl, Python) may give the false impression that the majority of OSSP are successful. The reality of these projects, however, is somehow different. A large number of them has actually been abandoned as they fail in attracting and retaining developers' devotion until the completion of the first software beta version (Ewusi-Mensah, 1997; Crowston et al., 2006; Stewart and Gosain, 2006). Studies of project activity have shown that OSSP may have very high levels of turnover (Von Hippel and Von Krogh, 2003). Only a very small number of projects is active and a much larger number is relatively static, resulting in a Pareto and power law distribution (Hunt and Johnson, 2002).

Depending on developers' behavior, the outcomes of a project can be dramatically different. Indeed, developers contribute from around the world, and coordinate their activity primarily by means of computer-mediated communications (CMC) that span traditional boundaries of place and ownership. Moreover, developers contribute to projects as volunteers, on an autonomous basis, deciding how and when to contribute to project development without working for a common organization. This collective effort of decentralized, self-directed, highly interactive developers often results in software that is relatively stable (Raymond, 1999; Kogut and Metiu, 2001). Yet, these same distinctive characteristics that differ largely from traditionally advocated software engineering practices make OSSP and their effectiveness largely dependent upon developers' behavior. Recognizing this critical need, many have called for a better understanding of *why and how software developers participate to these projects.*

This question is one of the fundamental research questions in OSSP as such projects are no longer considered to be early technical applications reserved for a category of products. Instead, today OSSP represent a wide variety of applications representing viable alternatives to proprietary systems. This implies that OSS is an expanding phenomenon in the computer software industry where developers' behavior, its antecedents and outcomes are key.

In response, the current study develops a theoretical and empirical understanding of motivations, behavior and outcomes of OSSP developers (Figure 4.1). The proposed theoretical constructs and research model (Figure 4.2) were examined through a field study based on a web-based questionnaire of SourceForge.net developers. Theory development based upon Fishbein and Ajzen's theory of planned behavior and Dweck and Leggett's social-cognitive approach to motivation offers new empirical insights about developers' motivations and how it affects their behavior and outcomes.

Figure 4.1   The motivations, behavior, outcomes framework

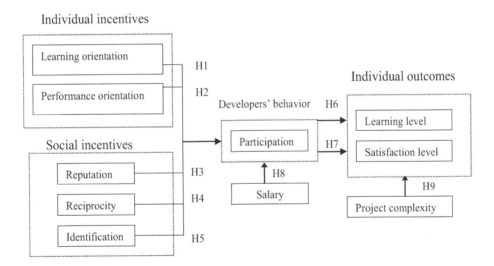

Figure 4.2   Research model

The proposed research model (Figure 4.2) integrates constructs from psychology and social exchange theories to explain developers' behavior in OSSP along with some of its associated outcomes. The basic concepts from psychology include motivations, which represent the impetus toward a behavior, in particular, individual incentives (i.e., learning and performance orientation) and social incentives (i.e., reputation, reciprocity, and identification). Developers' behavior, specifically, participation, represents a requisite to the performance of a behavior and is based on the widely used and accepted Theory of Reasoned Action (TRA) (Ajzen and Fishbein, 1980). According to Ajzen, the motivational factors that influence a behavior indicate how hard people are willing to try to perform the behavior in question. The stronger the motivations to carry out a behavior, the more likely the behavior will be carried out.

In our study, the most motivated developers will more likely behave stronger in terms of participation (contribution to the different activities of an OSSP) and the more likely will achieve performance outcomes at the individual level—learning and satisfaction outcomes. We describe each of the constructs, its relationships to developers' behavior, and its outcomes in the following sections.

THE DEPENDENT VARIABLE: DEVELOPERS' BEHAVIOR

Behavior is a resulting manner of acting, the outcome a person adopts in function of his/her own assimilation of different antecedents (Ajzen and Frisbein, 1980). In our study, these antecedents refer to two predictors outlined earlier: individual incentives (learning and performance orientation) and social incentives (reputation, reciprocity, and identification).

The Theory of Planned Behavior (Ajzen, 1991; Taylor and Todd, 1995) distinguishes between: *attitude, subjective norm* and *perceived behavioral control. Attitude* corresponds to positive or negative feelings about performing the target behavior (Fishbein and Ajzen, 1975). It influences intention to do a task ultimately the way the person behaves (Wixom and Todd, 2005, p. 86). *Subjective norm* is defined as "the person's perception that most people who are important to him think he should or should not perform the behavior in question" (Fishbein and Ajzen, 1975, p. 302). *Perceived behavioral control* corresponds to the "perceived ease or difficulty of performing the behavior" (Ajzen, 1991, p. 108). It can be assimilated to the *self-efficacy* concept defined in Social Cognitive Theory as judgment of one's ability to accomplish a specific task

(Compeau and Higgins, 1995). This implies that behavior is influenced mainly by two dimensions: social and individual.

Behavior involves both a subjective and an objective dimension. The subjective dimension represents a psychological state: how a person thinks and feels (e.g., positive or negative feelings). It's often conceptualized in terms of *involvement* and *attitude*. The objective dimension, on the other hand, reflects what actually people do. While both dimensions are important, in this research we focus on the actual behavior—*participation*—to be able to compare our results against previous studies which focused on this particular dimension of behavior.

INDEPENDENT VARIABLES

Prior preliminary research on motivations of OSS developers relied primarily on two theoretical models. The first stream focuses mainly on social exchange theory and social movement research (Blau, 1964). It builds, consequently, on the social dimension of developers' participation in OSSP. The second stream builds on the distinction between intrinsic and extrinsic motives and focuses particularly on individual rather than social motives (Deci and Ryan, 2000). We put forward this distinction by differentiating between individual and social incentives that shape developers' behavior in OSSP. This distinction is also consistent with the "private-collective" model of innovation incentives suggested by Von Hippel and Von Krogh (2003), arguing for the intermediary position of OSS models and the existing assumption in OSS studies that motivations are complementary or "mutually reinforcing" (e.g., Markus et al., 2000).

INDIVIDUAL INCENTIVES

Our research further suggests that the individual incentives that shape developers' behavior in OSSP can be articulated under two mains variables: learning orientation and performance expectancy. These variables may be related to the goal orientation motives that have roots in psychology. Although originally developed in the educational psychology literature to explain differences in student learning behavior (e.g., Diener and Dweck, 1978, 1980; Dweck and Reppucci, 1973), goal orientation has become one of the most frequently studied motivational variables in applied psychology and is currently the dominant approach in the study of achievement motivation.

Achievement motivation theory asserts that goals are the central determinants of behavior patterns.

Many studies have highlighted the role of goal orientation in shaping the behavioral patterns (e.g., Elliot and Dweck, 1988) exhibited by individuals in achievement-related settings. Goal orientation refers to "individual differences for goal preferences in achievement settings" (Van de Walle et al., 1999). According to the original theory and research by Nicholls (1984), Dweck and Elliot (1983), Dweck and Leggett (1988), there are two categories of goal orientation. In the first one, *performance goal orientation*, individuals are focused on the demonstration and verification of their ability that can be achieved by seeking favorable evaluations of their competence. In the other category, *learning goal orientation*, individuals are concerned with increasing their competence and the acquisition of new skills. OSSP are one of these settings where developers' behavior is shaped by their learning orientation and performance expectancy.

Learning orientation

Learning is considered one of the primary reasons developers join OSSP. OSSP represent an ideal context for developers to share knowledge, expertise, and technical crafts (Raymond, 1999; Kogut and Metiu, 2001; Lakhani and Von Hippel, 2003; Von Hippel and Von Krogh, 2003). Any developer can decide to participate through the open source platform to the software development process in order to enhance his or her competences in terms of programming. Developers in OSSP can learn new procedural and programming skills (Crowston et al., 2006). They can learn a new language, adopt from other participants professional rules to structure programs (i.e., how variables should be named, how functions and procedures need to be used, how programs can be developed in object-oriented methods, etc.), and enhance their technical skills by reusing and modifying prior open source programs.

This way of learning by doing is consistent with Brown and Duguid (1991) who consider learning as a process where learners are also practitioners. Learning by doing and deliberate investments in learning and making improvements is consequently an important dimension of the individual incentives that shape developers' behavior. We will refer to this dimension as *learning orientation*. Learning orientation refers to the disposition of individuals towards learning in the aim of enhancing their own competence and has roots in educational psychology (Dweck and Leggett, 1988). Individuals with a strong learning orientation believe their own skills and abilities can be improved, and thus they "persist, escalate effort, engage in solution-oriented self-instruction, and report enjoying the challenge" (Brett and Van de Walle, 1999, p. 864). This implies that developers join OSSP with the aim of learning and developing their skills and competences. Based on this, we hypothesize that:

> H1: Developers' learning orientation positively influences their behavior in OSSP.

Performance expectancy

Apart from the learning orientation, developers' behavior in OSSP is also shaped by their performance expectancy. Indeed, Dweck (1990) notes that a person may operate in both systems of learning and performance goals. Developers with high performance expectancy seek to demonstrate to themselves and to others their ability and competence. Performance expectancy in the IS context has been defined as the "degree to which an individual believes that using the system will help him or her to attain gains in job performance" (2003, p. 449). It includes perceived usefulness, relative advantage, and outcome expectations. In the context of our study, developers may join OSSP to demonstrate to themselves—and to others—their level of ability and establish the adequacy of their ability in the eyes of other developers.

> H2: Developers' performance expectancy positively influences their behavior in OSSP.

SOCIAL INCENTIVES

While the individual motives of developers to participate in OSSP find their roots in psychology. Several other motives to participate in OSSP are derived from developers' desire to be part of a community and gain benefits as social actors. These incentives find their roots in social exchange theory that views the exchange relationship between specific actors as "actions contingent on rewarding reactions from others" (Blau, 1964, p. 91). In particular we focus on three dimensions of social incentives: *identification, reciprocity* and *reputation*.

Identification

A first form of incentives for OSS developers is related to the identity represented by belonging to an OSSP. Identification or "identity" indicates affiliation to a particular social group. As Tajfel puts it: "social identity is the individual's knowledge that he belongs to a certain social group together with some emotional or value significance to him of this group membership" (Tajfel, 1972, p. 292; Hogg and Terry, 2000, p. 122). In this definition, two elements can be distinguished: the first component conveys the extent to which an individual perceives him/herself as belonging to the group, being interwined with the fate of the group, and being a typical member of it. The second component is related to a feeling of pride of belonging to the organization or feeling acknowledged in the organization (Tajfel, 1972, p. 24). This component is strongly related to the self-enhancement motive. While the latter dimension of identification is mainly tied to the organization it can clearly refer to a group or community.

In the context of OSSP, the team's beliefs are the glue that holds developers together. These beliefs guide the specific means by which OSS development is conducted, and in some cases may provide, according to Stewart and Gosain (2006), an explanation of behaviors enacted by team members that might otherwise be interpreted negatively. This social influence exerted by the open source community is essential for software projects to be developed and to persist without a central authority or commercial objectives (Scacchi et al., 2006). This community dimension of OSSP has been analyzed in several articles (Gallivan, 2001; Gosain, 2003). Adhering to and sharing ideological principles shapes developers' behavior in OSSP. Stewart and Gosain (2006) distinguish between norms, values and beliefs. Beliefs are the basic assumptions referring to the underlying philosophy of the community and belong to our conceptualization of identification. They include, for instance, the belief that the quality of the code produced is higher when its open and freely available than when it is privately developed for commercial purposes, and the belief that bugs are more rapidly fixed when anybody is able to meddle than when they are performed by closed teams of developers. Based on this, we hypothesize that:

> H3: The higher the level of identification of developers with OSSP the higher their participation level.

Reciprocity

Beyond belonging to a particular "ideology," developers' behavior in OSSP is also shaped by other social incentives, in particular, reciprocity. Reciprocity refers to the sense that an individual contribution to a community is done with the expectancy that other participants will behave in the same way in response (Shumaker and Brownell, 1984). With difference to game theory, it does not mean a one-to-one reciprocity expectation but refers mainly to its collective dimension: "behave with the community members like I did with you." Reciprocity is a way to perpetrate the stability of cooperation and to develop and maintain trust over time (Arrow, 1974).

On this point, electronic networks sharply contrast with traditional communities of practice where day-to-day social life is characterized by face-to-face exchanges enforcing expectation of reciprocity through social sanctions (Wasko and Faraj, 2005, p. 37). OSS communities can be better considered as a "network of practice" where individuals are coordinated through an electronic platform and while sharing knowledge and experiences may never meet each other face to face (Brown and Duguid, 2000). The social capital of a community is not likely to be fully recovered when transferred in an electronic network of practice (Lin, 2001; Putnam, 1995). For instance, in electronic networks, participants have no control over other participants' responses on the forum and no assurance that they will not act like a "free rider" or will help in return by also contributing to the project. Moreover, electronic networks of practice, like open source communities, would simply disappear if there were too many free riders. This reinforces the relevance of a satisfactory reciprocity that shapes developers' behavior in OSSP.

H4: Reciprocity positively influences developers' behavior in OSSP.

Reputation

Social exchange theory recognizes that actors engaged in social relations may also expect other rewards like respect, reputation or recognition (Blau, 1964). For OSSP developers, building their reputation means gaining respect from peers (Nichols and Twidale, 2002). A developer's contributions to an OSSP play a key role in how he/she is perceived in the community and results in building a reputation. Lerner and Tirole (2002) find that those who contributed code also gained private benefits by signaling to prospective employers about their programming skills and thereby getting better career opportunities. In this way, like "freelance" developers, participants of an OSSP look for some professional experiences allowing them to show off their talent and abilities and establish a reputation. In OSSP, seeking to maintain or enhance reputation can affect developers' behavior. Accordingly, we suggest that:

H5: Reputation positively influences developers' behavior in OSSP.

PERFORMANCE OUTCOMES

Learning outcomes

In addition to influencing the behavioral responses of developers in OSSP, learning orientation also shapes individual cognitive response patterns towards the work they perform (Dweck and Leggett, 1988). Learning orientation has been suggested to affect learning outcomes by improving the utilization of existing knowledge and changing the manner in which day-to-day work is conducted. Because individuals with a strong learning orientation invest more attention in learning, they are more likely to extract new knowledge from the activities they are already performing.

Recent findings from an empirical analysis of OSSP find both knowledge creation and transfer to be possible in this context (Hemetsberger and Reinhardt, 2006). These authors explain that some functionalities available online compensate for the absence of face-to-face interactions. For instance, commentaries added in code programs and concurrent version systems (CVS) allow developers to review the process that lies behind the code developed by others. Enabling developers to review the whole history of code development allows them, consequently, to be engaged in reflective observation and to learn from the improvements and errors made previously. This implies that developers with a strong learning orientation will develop a more positive behavior toward OSSP and their learning outcomes will be as a result higher. To distinguish learning outcome levels, we based our analysis on three dimensions put forward by Hogg and Terry (2000). The first one, *replication*, refers to mastering techniques and methods necessary to carry out one's daily work tasks. The second one, *adaptation*, is related to the ability of a person to update their knowledge in order to adapt their resolution mode to environmental changes. The last one, *innovation*, corresponds to the attitude of a person who transforms their cognitive schemes and creates new resolution modes representing a significant added value in problem solving.

> H6a: Developers with a positive behavior acquire replication abilities from the OSSP.

> H6b: Developers with a positive behavior acquire adaptation abilities from the OSSP.

H6c: Developers with a positive behavior acquire innovation abilities from the OSSP.

Satisfaction outcomes

Apart from the learning outcomes outlined above, our research considers developers' satisfaction as an important dimension in the outcomes they achieve (Crowston et al., 2006). The most motivated developers will have a positive behavior towards OSSP and their satisfaction with these projects will be as a result higher. Developers' satisfaction may entail different dimensions. A developer can be more or less satisfied with the outcome of the project itself. Taking into account this dimension is of critical importance as several OSSP are abandoned before their closure, or result in outcomes that differ largely from initially assigned objectives (Scacchi et al., 2002).

Indeed, several OSSP evolve in a way by which the software finally developed serves other needs than the ones of the initiator of the project (Roberts et al., 2004). The absence of a central authority in project teams, of formal deadlines and monetary rewards implies that developers have an important autonomy in fulfilling their tasks. Thus, beyond defined project objectives, developers can afford to decide themselves what modules should be developed or not with regards to their perceived interests in the open source community. In the same vein, OSS developers' satisfaction depends also on their social experience with the project team. Based on this, we hypothesize that:

H7a: Developers with a positive behavior towards OSSP will be more satisfied with the project outcomes.

H7b: Developers with a positive behavior towards OSSP will be more satisfied with the OSS team.

CONTROL VARIABLES

We used two control variables in our model of Motivations–Behavior–Outcomes of OSSP: *salary*—whether developers are paid to participate in a particular project—and *project complexity*—the variability in complexity of OSSP.

Salary

As the number of developers sponsored by companies for their contributions to OSSP is increasing, controlling how this dimension affects developers' behavior is of particular importance. This tendency is confirmed by recent studies which find 30 per cent to 54 per cent of OSSP contributors to be paid at least in part for their work (Lakhani et al., 2002; Hertel et al., 2003). Such distortions to the unpaid participation principle by which the open source community has been set up and often operates should not be neglected. The literature in psychology for instance, highlights *extrinsic rewards* (e.g., pay) potential to positively influence *intrinsic motivation* and the way individuals perform the tasks they are assigned to (Hennesey and Amabile, 1998).

In open source, however, the case study of Roberts et al. (2004) revealed that being paid was positively related to developers' *status/opportunity motivations* and *participation* while negatively related to their *use value motivations*. In this study, we expect that individuals who are being paid to contribute to OSSP are likely to have a more positive behavior, in terms of participation, than those who are not paid.

> H8: Being paid to participate to OSSP is positively related to developers' behavior.

Project complexity

Information systems development is generally acknowledged to be an intellectually complex activity (Benbya and McKelvey, 2006). This complexity is not only due to complex tasks demanding more cues (Speier et al., 2003), information manipulation (Shaw, 1976) and, consequently, more dependencies between processes (Wood, 1986). But it is also a result of group interactions (Waltz et al., 1993). Indeed, most of the software applications developed today are extremely sophisticated and require an extensive integration of different knowledge domains. This is particularly significant in the case of OSSP, which can have a high variability of complexity likely to influence some of the results observed. We therefore, hypothesize that:

> H9: Developers' performance outcomes is influenced by OSSP complexity.

3. Research Methodology and Data Collection

This section describes our research approach, instrument development, and data collection processes. To test the proposed research model, we adopted the survey method for data collection, and examined our hypotheses by applying the partial least squares (PLS) method to the collected data. Our unit of analysis, as outlined earlier is the individual developer.

The majority of research in OSS has focused on case studies such as Linux and Apache (e.g., Gallivan, 2001, Mockus et al., 2002, Bagozzi and Dholakia, 2006). Even if these projects are interesting and important, they may not be representative of the majority of OSSP in terms of technology, importance, team size, and funding, among other dimensions (Stewart and Gosain, 2006). Thus, developing studies with different OSSP characteristics compared to Linux and Apache can support or disprove the results found from previous studies. This approach is more representative of the wider population of OSS.

We, consequently, collected data related to OSSP hosted on SourceForge (www.SourceForge.net). We have chosen SourceForge first because it is the world's largest repository of OSS development. SourceForge has today more than 180,000 projects and more than 1.9 million registered users. Second, SourceForge.net provides free hosting to OSS development projects. Third, SourceForge's mission is to enrich the open source community by providing a centralized infrastructure for developers to control and manage OSS development (managing projects, issues, communications, and code). Therefore, SourceForge provides these projects with a standard technology toolset, reducing variance in developer behavior that may be due to differences in technology used to support workflow, code distribution, versioning, etc.

Our unit of analysis is the OSS developer working on a specific software application. It is recognized that only those individuals who have a high degree of development skills in OSS would be able to comment knowledgeably about the importance of developer behavior. Thus, given the practical difficulty of accessing all members of an OSSP, administrators of these projects were chosen as "key informants." The use of key informants requires a deliberate strategy to access respondents that possess special qualifications pertinent to the research such as status, experience, or specialized knowledge (Segars and Grover, 1998). We targeted project administrators as they are the best positioned to provide the requisite perspective and select developers to further participate to the survey. As study participants, in our case software developers, can function in the role of either respondent or informant (Seidler, 1974), preliminary decisions about the selection of study participants were based on consideration of the role assumed.

We further targeted software developers as they function as singular members of an OSSP to provide data that reflect their own personal perceptions (Kumar et al., 1993). Developers are the best positioned to report on their individual and social motives, and their influence on their behavior and outcomes. This data inherently provide measurement at the individual unit of analysis because they are bound to the opinions, attitudes, or beliefs of each respondent (Anderson, 1987).

Data was collected using two surveys from the SourceForge website. The first survey included open-ended questions asking project administrators about the way they are developing code freely. Administrators of 100 SourceForge most downloaded projects were contacted using email; 34 administrators completed the questionnaire. The qualitative data collected on this survey was then used to develop the wording of social and individual incentives, developers' behavior and learning and satisfaction outcomes to be included on a second survey for hypotheses testing.

A different set of projects was targeted for the second survey. We selected projects from different categories in different domains listed in SourceForge. A criterion to choose among projects in different categories was project activity and maturity. We ensured that the projects had some activity in the past week in terms of contributions to the code repository; requests for bug-fixes, support, patches or features; or in terms of page views. And we selected projects that were listed as mature projects to understand why developers participate in this category of projects. In total, 150 projects met all criteria. A subset of these projects was randomly selected to pilot test the survey. We have selected in each project, the member of the project where the role/position was stated as developer. In total, those projects led to 834 specific email addresses. For the pilot test, we targeted developers and asked them to complete all Likert scale items, answer open-ended questions, and report if any of the items were unclear, if they had problems understanding or answering any questions, or if there were ways the survey itself could be improved. Twelve developers responded, and none of them indicated any problems in the survey. Personalized invitations were then sent to the remaining developers in the sample requesting their participation. In all, 230 developers responded to our survey from a sample size of 822 (an overall response rate of 28 per cent).

OPERATIONALIZATION OF CONSTRUCTS

The questionnaire used to measure developers' behavior, its antecedents and outcomes, comprised items for measuring the degree to which individual and social incentives impact developers' behavior in OSSP and their performance outcomes. All the items were measured using a standard five-point Likert scale ranging from 1 = Strongly Disagree to 5 = Strongly Agree. Our measurement instrument uses previously developed scales for measuring the different variables derived from literature reviews and academic research.

A literature review was conducted to locate past operational measures of the constructs under investigation and groups of questions were compiled from validated instruments to represent each construct. The wording of the identified measures was modified to fit the OSS context of this study.

As outlined earlier, we focus mainly on the objective dimension of behavior: *participation*. To measure participation in OSSP we used the list of activities defined by Zhao and Deek (2004). It defines *participation* as the level of contribution to the following activities: find bugs, find usability problems, suggest new features, review and inspect source code, submit source code. These different activities have been confirmed by our key informants. As for individual incentives, *learning orientation* and *performance expectancy* have been adapted from Dweck and Leggett (1998) to fit the OSS context of this study. We measured *identity* using four items adapted from Stewart and Gosain (2006). *Reciprocity* was measured with four items adapted from Bandura (1995). And *Reputation* was measured with four items. The learning outcomes were measured with six items adapted from Hogg and Terry (2000): two items for *replication*, two for *adaptation*, and two for *innovation*. Finally, *satisfaction outcomes* were measured with five items: three items reflect the satisfaction with the project and its outcomes and two items refer to the satisfaction with the team.

4. Results Analysis

Data were analyzed using Partial Least Square (PLS), a structural equation modeling technique that employs principal component analysis, path analysis, and regression to simultaneously evaluate data and theory. PLS allows to both specify the relationships among the conceptual factors of interest and the measures underlying each construct, resulting in a simultaneous analysis of (1) how well the measures relate to each construct and (2) whether the hypothesized relationships at the theoretical level are empirically true. PLS was used because it is more appropriate than alternatives, such as LISREL and AMOS, when sample size are small, models are complex, the goal of the research is to explain the variance, and the measures are not well established (Fornell and Bookstein, 1982). We first examined the measurement model which includes the *reliability and discriminant validity* of the measures, then the *structural model*. The rationale of this two-step approach was to ensure that our conclusion on structural relationships was drawn from a set of measurement instruments with desirable properties. The two-step analytical procedures for PLS analysis were allowed (Hair et al., 1998). Concerning the assessment of the measurement model, individual item loadings and internal consistency were examined with a test of reliability. Individual item loadings and internal consistencies with the Cronbach Alpha are greater than 0.72 (see Table 4.1), thus are considered adequate (Fornell and Larcker, 1981), and all the weights are statistically significant at $p<0.001$. The uniformity of the distribution of the weights shows that each item contributes to each construct equally.

Table 4.1   Summary of constructs

Construct Name	Construct identifier	Cronbach Alpha	Number of items	Number of items carried forward the analysis	AVE	CR
Learning orientation	LEA	0.89	3	3	0.82	0.94
Performance expectancy	PER	0.72	2	2	0.73	0.88
Reputation	REP	0.75	4	3	0.76	0.84
Identity	IDE	0.73	4	3	0.72	0.82
Reciprocity	REC	0.88	4	4	0.73	0.92
Participation	PAR	0.75	5	5	0.67	0.88
Adaptation	ADA	0.81	2	2	0.84	0.91
Replication	REP	0.90	2	2	0.91	0.95
Innovation	INN	0.72	2	2	0.79	0.88
Team satisfaction	TES	0.87	2	2	0.88	0.94
Project satisfaction	PRS	0.83	3	3	0.78	0.91
Project complexity	PRO	0.74	4	3	0.72	0.87

RELIABILITY AND VALIDITY

One measure of reliability using confirmatory factor analysis used here is the composite reliability (CR) (Fornell and Larcker, 1981). This measure has frequently been used to test model reliability (Raghunathan et al., 1999). The composite reliability, which reflects the internal consistency of the indicators, ranges from 0.82 to 0.95 for the constructs indicating a high internal consistency (these statistics are shown in Table 4.1).

We can also use the average variance extracted (AVE) to measure the amount of variance that a construct captures from its indicators relative to the variance contained in measurement error. All AVEs for the constructs used in this study are greater than 0.67, which indicates that more than 67 per cent of the variance of the indicators can be accounted for by the latent variables (Table 4.1). The AVE can be interpreted as both a measure of reliability for the construct and as a means of evaluating discriminant validity (Fornell and Larcker, 1981). For the case of the discriminant validity assessment, the AVEs should be greater than the square of the correlations among the constructs, which corresponds to the amount of variance shared between a latent variable and its block of indicators that should be greater than shared variance between the latent variables. In this study, the square root of each AVE value is greater than the off-diagonal elements (Table 4.1). The results indicate reasonable discriminant validity among all of the constructs.

STRUCTURAL MODEL

We tested our hypotheses by examining the size and significance of structural paths in the PLS analysis and the percentage of variance explained (see Figure 4.3). The results of our analyses provide support for the role of the individual — learning orientation and performance expectancy — and social incentives — reputation, reciprocity and identification — on developer behavior and their effects on its performance outcomes — learning outcomes and satisfaction level. The empirical results support our hypotheses and reveal that the individual and social incentives suggested explain almost 50 per cent of the variation on developers' behavior ($R^2=0.496$). All of the paths in the model are statistically significant (at $p=0.001$ level).

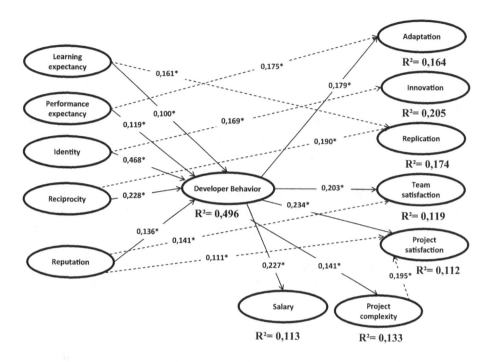

Figure 4.3   The structural model

We first examine the propositions relating individual and social incentives to developer behavior (H1, H2, H3, H4, H5; see Figure 4.2). The model explained 49.6 per cent of the variance in developer behavior. As hypothesized, learning orientation, (H1, $\beta = 0.1$, $p < 0.01$) and performance expectancy (H2, $\beta = 0.119$, $p < 0.01$) significantly and positively predicted developer behavior.

We also suggested that developer behavior in OSSP is shaped by social motives: reputation (H3), reciprocity (H4), and identification (H5). As hypothesized, these social motives have a positive and significant relationship with developer behavior ($\beta = 0.136$, $p < 0.01$; $\beta = 0.228$, $p < 0.01$; $\beta = 0.468$, $p < 0.01$) respectively. And by two other control variables: salary (H8) and project complexity (H9). We find the relationship between these two control variables and developer behavior to be positive and significant (H8, $\beta = 0.227$, $p < 0.01$; H9, $\beta = 0.141$).

Second, we analyze our hypotheses relating developer behavior to its learning and satisfaction outcomes. Concerning the effects of developer behavior on their satisfaction outcomes (H7), it has a strong and positive effect on both dimensions: team satisfaction ($\beta = 0.203$, $p < 0.01$) and project satisfaction ($\beta = 0.234$, $p < 0.01$). But its relationship with learning outcomes was supported mainly for adaptation.

5. Discussion

This study has examined the relationships between the motivations, behavior, and outcomes of OSS developers. Studies of OSS motivations have, in recent years, suggested a variety of reasons to explain why and how developers contribute to these projects. Their results, however, have not been entirely consistent. The mixed findings about the dominant motives and the shift the OSS movement is noticing these days provided the impetus to re-examine developers' motivations in OSSP.

Guided by seminal studies in achievement motivation theory, this study proposed two individual incentives to explain developers' behavior in OSSP and its associated outcomes: learning orientation and performance expectancy. As expected, both learning and performance orientation were positively associated with developer behavior. This suggests that one reason why developers participate to OSSP is to continually improve their skills. But they also participate to OSSP because they can compare themselves to other developers and by this way demonstrate to themselves and to others their level of ability.

This study suggests also three social motives to explain developers' behavior in OSSP: identity, reciprocity, and reputation. We find identity to be the strongest motive shaping developers' behavior in OSSP. This dimension has been suggested by several previous studies to explain developers' commitment and participation to OSSP (e.g., Stewart and Gosain, 2006). It refers to the ideological principles that developers believe in and that contributed largely to the emergence of the OSS movement. We also find the other two social motives: *reciprocity* and *reputation* to be the strongest predictors of developer behavior in OSSP than the individual motives outlines earlier. We finally suggested salary also as a predictor to developer behavior and we find that being paid is positively related to developer behavior.

Our findings, therefore, first reveal that developers have multiple motives to participate to OSSP, and that some motivations, specifically, the social motives, are more influential on their behavior than others. Within the social motives, identity accounts for (β =0.468), it is followed in importance by the reciprocity dimension (0.228) and then reputation (0.136). Second, despite the increasing number of organizations sponsoring OSSP and which leads one to expect that the motivations of developers today have evolved from ideological to more rational motives; our findings suggest that this is not the case. While, we find salary to be a significant dimension that shapes developers' behavior (R^2=0.113), its effect remains marginal compared to the social and individual motives suggested.

With regards to the outcomes dimension from OSSP, we find developers' motives and behavior to be associated both to satisfaction and learning outcomes.

One surprising finding related developer behavior with learning outcomes. We expected developer behavior to be related to three learning outcomes: innovation, replication, and adaptation. However, contrary to our predictions, developer behavior is associated positively to adaptation and was not significant to innovation and replication. These outcomes, however, were all largely significant when associated to developers' motives. One explanation of this finding is that participation of developer alone is not a driver of innovation. Innovation is recognized to be a complex mental process where improvisation, serendipity and determination play a key role. How developers' behavior in OSSP may drive innovation remains an open question for future studies.

Conclusion

This study makes several contributions to the OSS literature. First, it provides theoretical and empirical support of motivations, behavior and outcomes of developers in mature OSSP listed on SourceForge. While several studies have examined particular aspects of developers' motivations in OSSP, we are not aware of any study that has examined the different motives and their implications on developer's behavior and individual outcomes. Further, existing literature on OSS still presents conflicting evidence about the dominant motives of developers in OSSP.

Our results reveal interesting findings with regards to what motivates developers to contribute to mature OSSP. While one may expect rational motives—financial and performance or learning orientation—to drive developer behavior in OSSP and its associated outcomes, this research reveals the opposite. Our results indicate that the importance of these motives remains marginal compared to the motivation to belong to a community of members sharing the same basic values about the finality toward which software should be developed. The ideological principles that initially drove the OSS movement remain the primary motivation of developers' contributions to OSSP. Other social motives, specifically, reciprocity and reputation, are also important motivations of developers.

We also find that the individual incentives suggested, while less important than the social ones, are significant and positively associated to developer behavior. Developers are motivated as much by learning and performance orientation as they are by receiving a salary on their contribution. This particular finding has several research implications. First, while there's an increasing number of projects receiving funds and financial support, further empirical studies could be done on the effects of these extrinsic factors on the social and ideological motives that remain the main driver of developers' behavior. Second, while SourceForge is one of the most important OSS platforms, it's mainly used by a community of volunteers and other platforms are used by developers for commercial software owned and developed by a company sponsoring the project. Future research, may investigate how several "sub-OSS communities" may coexist and how they may differ in their motivations instead of one community like most research articles study.

References

Ajzen, I. (1991) The Theory of Planned Behavior, *Organizational Behavior and Human Decision Processes* (50), 179–211.

Ajzen, I. and Fishbein, M. (1980) *Understanding Attitudes and Predicting Social Behavior*, Englewood Cliffs, NJ: Prentice-Hall Inc.

Anderson, J. (1987), An Approach for Confirmatory Measurement and Structural Equation Modeling of Organizational Properties, *Management Science*, 33 (April), 525–41.

Arrow, K.J. (1974) *The Limits of Organization*, New York: W.W. Norton and Company.

Bagozzi, R. and Dholakia, U. (2006) Open Source Software User Communities: A Study of Participation in Linux User Groups, *Management Science* (52:7), 1099–115.

Bandura, A. (1995) Exercise of Personal and Collective Efficacy in Changing Societies, in A. Bandura (ed.) *Self-efficacy in Changing Societies*, New York: Cambridge University Press 1–45.

Benbya, H. and Belbaly. N. (2010) Understanding Developers' Motives in Open Source Projects: A Multi-Theoretical Framework. *Communications of the Association for Information Systems* (27:30).

Benbya, H. and McKelvey, B. (2006) Towards a Complexity Theory of Information Systems Development, *Information Technology and People* (19:1), 12–34.

Blau, P.M. (1964) *Exchange and Power in Social Life*, New York: Wiley.

Brett, F.J. and Van de Walle, D. (1999) Goal Orientation and Goal Content as Predictors of Performance in a Training Program, *Journal of Applied Psychology* (84), 863–73.

Brown, J.S. and Duguid, P. (1991) Organizational Learning and Communities-of-Practice: Toward a Unified View of Working, Learning, and Innovation, *Organization Science* (2:1), 40–57.

Brown, J.S. and Duguid, P. (2000) *The Social Life of Information*, Boston, MA: Harvard Business School Press.

Compeau, D.R. and Higgins, C.A. (1995) Application of Social Cognitive Theory to Training for Computer Skills, *Information Systems Research* (6:2), 118–42.

Crowston, K., Howison, J. and Annabi, H. (2006) Information Systems Success in Free and Open Source Software Development: Theory And Measures, *Software Process: Improvement and Practice* (special issue on free/open source software processes) 11, 123–48.

Davis, F. (1989) Perceived Usefulness, Perceived Ease of Use and User Acceptance of Information Technology, *MIS Quarterly* (13:3), 319–40.

Deci, E.L. and Ryan, R.M. (2000) The "What" and "Why" of Goal Pursuits: Human Needs and the Self-determination of Behavior. *Psychological Inquiry*, 11, 227–68.

Diener, C.I. and Dweck, C.S. (1978) An Analysis of Helplessness: Continuous Changes in Performance, Strategy and Achievement Cognitions Following Failure, *Journal of Personality and Social Psychology* (36), 451–62.

Diener, C.I. and Dweck, C.S. (1980) An Analysis of Learned Helplessness II. The Processing of Success, *Journal of Personality and Social Psychology* (39), 940–52.

Dweck, C.S. (1990) *Self-theories and Goals: Their Role in Motivation, Personality, and Development*. Lincoln, NE: University of Nebraska Press.

Dweck, C.S. and Elliott, E.S. (1983) Achievement Motivation, in P. Mussen and M. Hetherington (eds), *Handbook of Child Psychology (Vol. IV)*, New York: John Wiley, 643–91.

Dweck, C.S. and Leggett, E.L. (1988) A Social-cognitive Approach to Motivation and Personality, *Psychological Review* (95:2), 256–73.

Dweck, C.S. and Reppucci, N.D. (1973) Learned Helplessness and Reinforcement Responsibility in Children, *Journal of Personality and Social Psychology* (25), 109–16.

Elliott, E.S. and Dweck, C.S. (1988) Goals: An Approach to Motivation and Achievement, *Journal of Personality and Social Psychology* (54:1), 5–12.

Ewusi-Mensah, K. (1997) Critical Issues in Abandoned Information Systems Development Projects, *Communication of the ACM* (40:9), 74–80.

Fishbein, M. and Ajzen, I. (1975) *Belief, Attitude, Intentions and Behavior: An Introduction to Theory and Research*, Boston, MA: Addison-Wesley.

Fornell, C. and Bookstein, F.L. (1982) Two Structural Equation Models: LISREL and PLS Applied to Consumer Exit-voice Theory, *Journal of Marketing Research* (19:4), 440–52.

Fornell, C. and Larcker, D.F. (1981) Structural Equation Models With Unobservable Variables and Measurement Error: Algebra and Statistics, *Journal of Marketing Research* (18:3), 382–8.

Gallivan, M.J. (2001) Striking a Balance between Trust and Control in a Virtual Organization, *Information Systems Journal* (11), 277–304.

Ghosh, R. et al. (2002) *Survey of Developers. Free/Libre and Open Source Software: Survey and Study*. Final report. International Institute of Infonomics, Berlecom Research GmbH.

Gosain, S. (2003) Looking through a Window on Open Source Culture: Lessons for Community Infrastructure Design, *Systèmes d'Information et Management* (8:1), 11–42.

Hair, J.F., Anderson, R.E., Tatham, R.L. and Black, W.C. (1998) *Multivariate Data Analysis with Readings*, Englewood Cliffs, NJ: Prentice Hall.

Hann, I.-H., Roberts, J. and Slaughter, S. (2006) Understanding the Motivations, Participation, and Performance of Open Source Software Developers: A Longitudinal Study of the Apache Projects, *Management Science* (52:7), July, 984–99.

Hars, A. and Ou, S. (2002) Working for Free? Motivations for Participating in Open Source Projects, *International Journal of Electronic Commerce*, (6:3), 25–39.

Hemetsberger, A. and Reinhardt, C. (2006) Learning and Knowledge-building in Communities, *Management Learning* (37:2), 187–214.

Hennessey, B.A. and Amabile, T.M. (1998) Reward, Intrinsic Motivation, and Creativity, *American Psychologist* (53:6), 674–5.

Hertel, G., Neidner, S. and Hermann, S. (2003) Motivation of Software Developers in Open Source Projects: an Internet-based Survey of Contributors to the Linux Kernel, *Research Policy* (32:7), 1159–77.

Hogg, M.A. and Terry, D.J. (2000) Social Identity and Self-Categorization Processes in Organizational Contexts, *Academy of Management Review* (25:1) 121–40.

Hunt, F. and Johnson, P. (2002) On the Pareto Distribution of Open Source Projects, *Proceedings of the Open Source Software Development Workshop*, Newcastle.

Kogut, B. and Metiu, A. (2001) Open Source Software Development and Distributed Innovation, *Oxford Rev. Econom. Policy* (17:2), 248–64.

Kumar, N., Stern, L.W. and Anderson, J.C. (1993) Conducting Interorganizational Research using Key Informants, *Academy of Management Journal* (36:6), 1633–52.

Lakhani, K. and Von Hippel, E. (2003) How Open Source Software Works: Free User-to-user Assistance, *Research Policy* (32:6), 923–43.

Lakhani, K. and Wolf, R. (2005) Why Hackers Do What They Do: Understanding Motivation and Effort in Free/Open Source Software Projects. In Feller, J.R. et al. (eds), *Perspectives on Free and Open Source Software*. Cambridge, MA: MIT Press.

Lakhani, K., Wolf, B., Bates, J. and DiBona, C. (2002) The Boston Consulting Group Hacker Survey, Release 0.73, Boston MA. Available at http://www.osdn.com/bcg/bcg-0.73/BCGHackerSurveyv0-73.html.

Lerner, J. and Tirole, J. (2002) The Simple Economics of Open Source, *Journal of Industrial Economics*, 52, 197–234.

Lin, N. (2001) *Social Capital*, Cambridge: Cambridge University Press.

Markus, M.L., Manville, B. and Agres, C.E. (2000) What Makes a Virtual Organization Work?, *Sloan Management Review* (42:1), 13–26.

Mockus, A., Fielding, R. and Herbsleb, J.D. (2002) Two Case Studies of Open Source Software Development: Apache and Mozilla, *ACM Transactions on Software Engineering and Methodology* (11:3) 309–46.

Nicholls, J.G. (1984) Achievement Motivation: Conceptions of Ability, Subjective Experience, Task Choice, and Performance, *Psychological Review* (91), 328–46.

Nichols, D. and Twidale, M. (2002) *Usability and Open Source Software*, Working Paper 10/02, Department of Computer Science – University of Waikato.

Putnam, R. (1995) Bowling Alone: America's Declining Social Capital, *Journal of Democracy* (6:1), 65–78.

Raghunathan, B., Raghunathan, T.S. and Qiang, T. (1999) Dimensionality of the Strategic Grid Framework: The Construct and its Measurement, *Information Systems Research* (10:4), 343–55.

Raymond, E.S. (1999) *The Cathedral and the Bazaar. Musings on Linux and Open Source by an Accidental Revolutionary*, Sebastopol, CA: O'Reilly and Associates.

Roberts, T.L., Cheney, P.H., Sweeney, P.D. and Hightower, R.T. (2004) The Effects of Information Technology Project Complexity on Group Interaction, *Journal of Management Information System* (21:3), 223–47.

Riehle, D. (2007) The Economic Motivation of Open Source Software: Stakeholder Perspectives, *IEEE Computer* (4): 25–32.

Scacchi, W. (2002) Understanding the Requirements for Developing Open Source Software Systems, *IEE Proceedings Software* (149:1), 24–39.

Scacchi, W., Feller, J., Fitzgerald, B., Hissam, S. and Lakhani, K. (2006) Understanding Free/Open Source Software Development Processes, *Software Process—Improvement and Practice*.

Segars, A.H. and Grover, V. (1998) Strategic Information Systems Planning Success: an Investigation of the Construct and its Measurement, *MIS Quarterly* (22:2), 139–63.

Seidler, J. (1974) On Using Informants: a Technique for Collecting Quantitative Data and Controlling Measurement in Organization Analysis, *American Sociological Review* (39:6), 816–31.

Shah, S.K. (2006) Motivation, Governance, and the Viability of Hybrid Forms. *Management Science* (52:7), 1000–14.

Shaw, M.H. (1976) *Group Dynamics: The Psychology of Small Group Behavior*, New York: McGraw-Hill,.

Shumaker, S. and Brownell, A. (1984) Toward a Theory of Social Support: Closing Conceptual Gaps, *Journal of Social Issues* (40:4), 11–36.

Speier, C., Vessey, I. and Valacich, J.S. (2003) The Effects of Interruptions, Task Complexity, and Information Presentation on Computer-Supported Decision-Making Performance, *Decision Sciences* (34:4), 771–97.

Stallman R., Open Source: Voices from the Open Source Revolution, in Di-Bona, C., Ockman, S. and Stone, M. (eds.), *The GNU Operating System and the Free Software Movement*, Sebastopol, CA: O'Reilly.

Stewart, K.J. and Gosain, S. (2006) The Impact of Ideology on Effectiveness in Open Source Software Development Teams, *MIS Quarterly* (30:2), 291–314.

Tajfel, H. (1972) Experiments in a Vacuum, in Israel, J. and Tajfel, H. (eds), *The Context of Social Psychology*, London: Academic Press.

Taylor, S. and Todd, P. (1995) Understanding Information Technology Usage: A Test of Competing Models, *Information Systems Research* (6:2), 144–76.

Tetlock, P.E. (2000) Cognitive Biases and Organizational Correctives: Do Both Disease and Cure Depend on the Politics of the Beholder? *Administrative Science Quarterly* (45:2), 293–326.

Van de Walle, D., Brown, S.P., Cron, W.L. and Slocum, J.J.W. (1999) The Influence of Goal Orientation and Self-Regulation Tactics on Sales Performance: A Longitudinal Field Test, *Journal of Applied Psychology* (84:2), 249–59.

Venkatesh, V. and Davis, F. (2000) A Theoretical Extension of the Technology Acceptance Model: Four Longitudinal Field Studies, *Management Science* (46:2), 186–204.

Von Hippel, E. and Von Krogh, G. (2003) Open Source Software and the Private-Collective Innovation Model, *Organisation Science* (14:2), 209–23.

Vroom, D.J. and Jago, A.G. (1998) *The New Leadership. Managing Participation in Organizations*, Englewood Cliffs, NJ: Prentice Hall.

Waltz, D.B. Elam. J.J. and Cunis, B. (1993) Inside a Software Design Team: Knowledge Acquisition, Sharing, and Integration, *Communications of the ACM* (36:10), 62–80.

Wasko, M. and Faraj, S. (2005) Why Should I Share? Examining Social Capital And Knowledge Contribution in Electronic Networks of Practice, *MIS Quarterly* (29:1), 35–57.

Wixom, B.H. and Todd P.A. (2005) A Theoretical Integration of User Satisfaction and Technology Acceptance, *Information Systems Research* (6:1), 85–102.

Wood, R.E. (1986) Task Complexity: Definition of the Construct, *Organizational Behavior and Human Decision Processes* (37), 60–82.

Ye, Y., Nakajoki, K., Yamamoto, Y. and Kishida, K. (2004) The Co-Evolution of Systems and Communities in Free and Open Source Software Development, in S. Koch (ed.), *Free/Open Source Software Development*, Hershey, PA: Idea Group Publishing.

Zhao, L. and Deek, F. (2004) User Collaboration in Open Source Software Development, *Electronic Markets* (14:2), 89–103.

5

Social Capital in OSS Communities: A Cross-Level Research Model

JiJie Wang and Dan Robey

Introduction

Open source software (OSS) is a category of software under special licences that protect users' rights to access and modify the source code. The success of OSS projects, such as Linux operating systems, Apache web server and the BIND domain name resolution utility software, has impressed software users and sparked interests of scholars in academia. The development process for OSS is different from that of commercial software. In OSS, development work is not coordinated by organizational superstructure; rather, it is coordinated by community governance mechanisms. An estimated 70 per cent of OSS developers are volunteers, contributing to projects without direct economic compensation (Lakhani et al., 2002). The process of OSS development illustrates a new model of innovation creation, the so-called 'private-collective model', in which people devote private investments to innovation creation while providing the end product freely to all in the form of public goods (von Hippel and von Krogh, 2003; Jeppesen and Frederiksen, 2006).

It is essential for the OSS community to be sustainable if software users are to benefit continuously from OSS and the private-collective model of innovation creation. The sustainability of the OSS community, in turn, depends on the individual developer's continued contributions to the project and on users' acceptance and use of OSS products (Shah, 2006). Explaining why individuals contribute to the creation of public goods is an interesting question that has attracted considerable theoretical and empirical attention in the OSS literature and beyond (Hars and Ou, 2000; Ireland et al., 2002; Hann et al., 2003; Ye and Kishida, 2003; Hann et al., 2004). However, the focus on *individual* motivations belies the stated importance of *community* influences in OSS governance. For this reason, we develop a theoretical model showing the relationships between community characteristics, specifically social capital, and individual motivations and contributions to OSS projects. Our aims are not only to redress the imbalance in the literature toward individual-level analysis, but also to advance the conceptual understanding of social capital and its implications for community governance. Our model explains how social capital is accrued as a by-product of individual contributions and how social capital affects the motivation and contributions of community members.

We begin by reviewing literature on OSS projects and communities and theories of social capital. We then articulate the model and its three propositions. We illustrate each proposition using the Apache web server case as reported in prior research (Fielding, 1999; Mockus et al., 2000; Franke and von Hippel, 2003; Lakhani and von Hippel, 2003; Hann et al., 2004; Yan et al., 2005; Roberts et al., 2006). Although these studies do not discuss social capital explicitly, they provide insights supportive of the model's proposed theoretical relationships. This form of empirical support has been used in prior studies of OSS projects (Dinh-Trong and Bieman, 2005). Although the supporting studies can by no means be considered as empirical tests of the model, the literature engenders confidence in the model, which must ultimately be subjected to rigorous testing in future research.

Background

OPEN SOURCE SOFTWARE PROJECTS AND COMMUNITIES

OSS projects are often initiated by an individual developer or a small group of developers who want to develop software to solve problems that they encounter in life or work. After the essential components of the software are developed, the software and its source code are made available to others through the internet. Other software developers are attracted to make contributions to software development. OSS developers are mainly volunteers who do not get direct economic compensation. The levels of contributions vary among developers. Based on the theory of legitimate peripheral participation (Lave and Wenger, 1991) and observation of an OSS community, Ye and Kishida (2003) argued that OSS developers experienced role transformation as they contributed to development. When they joined the community, they assumed peripheral roles, such as passive user or bug reporter. As they increased their contributions, they moved toward the centre of the community and assumed more important roles, such as active developer or even core developer. A similar classification of community roles has been proposed for OSS users (Jin et al., 2007). Bonded by their shared interest in using and/or developing a particular OSS product, these developers together with users create an OSS community (Ye and Kishida, 2003).

The governance and coordination mechanisms within OSS communities are flexible, or even chaotic to some extent (Raymond, 1999). Developers working on the same project are normally geographically distributed, rarely meet face to face and communicate primarily through internet channels. Developers are not assigned to specific tasks, but pick the tasks they want to work on. Developers submit their software patches to the community. The submitted work first goes through peer review, and then the project leaders decide what to include in the released version of the software. Under the private-collective model of innovation creation, OSS developers invest their private resources to create novel software code and distribute it as a public good, freely available to all (von Hippel and von Krogh, 2003).

Less is known about the users of OSS products. However, it is important to include them as members of the OSS community for several reasons. First, OSS users vastly outnumber OSS developers. In 2004, the Linux operating system had 50,000 developers and 18 million users.[1] In 2000, Apache web server software had a comparatively small group of 15 core developers, 400 code contributors and 3,060 bug reporters, yet a huge penetration into the user community, with 65 per cent of the worldwide market (Mockus et al., 2000). The Mozilla community consists of 25 core developers, about 400 code contributors, 10,000 bug reporters, but over 500,000 users (Dotzler, 2003). Second, OSS users are important contributors to specific OSS projects. Although they may not contribute to core development, they are the most frequent reporters of bugs because software errors are most often detected in use. In addition, users may contribute end-user applications that other users find valuable. For example, OSS users may contribute developed applications based on OSS kernels free to other organizations. Beaumont Hospital in Ireland is one organization that has expressed interest in such developments, committing to make their staff fostering and tissue-matching systems available to other users (Fitzgerald and Kenny, 2004). Finally, OSS projects benefit from having more users because

---

1   http://zdnet.com.com/2100-1107_2-5073866.html.

they bring notoriety and ancillary commercial resources to projects, in turn enhancing the reputations of core developers (Jin et al., 2007).

INDIVIDUAL MOTIVATIONS TO CONTRIBUTE TO OSS COMMUNITIES

Hars and Ou (2000) identified three main categories of factors leading to participation in OSS projects: intrinsic motivation, personal needs and expectations of future returns. First, OSS developers are intrinsically motivated to participate in OSS. Some developers enjoy the process of programming; others feel the urge to increase other people's welfare by writing useful programs and helping users. Many people motivated by intrinsic needs may be considered 'hobbyists' (Shah, 2006). Second, developers contribute to OSS development out of their personal needs for the software (Roberts et al., 2006), and users provide assistance to others' learning more effective ways to use OSS (Lakhani and von Hippel, 2003). As mentioned by Raymond (1999, p. 32) 'Every good work of software starts by scratching a developer's personal itch.' The third category of motivation is expectation of future returns. Although volunteers are not directly compensated for their efforts, participation in some OSS projects does include financial compensation (Roberts et al., 2006), suggesting extrinsic motivations for participation. Even volunteers can potentially increase their future economic return by attaining status in an OSS project. Reputations gained within the OSS community can increase the chance of higher future compensation in the commercial software industry (Hann et al., 2003).

In summary, people are motivated for various reasons to contribute to OSS development. Although prior research has generated different categories of motivation, a close look reveals that the differences lie within the granularity of the categorization. In our model, we adopt the categorization of motives by Hars and Ou (2000) because it provides coverage of the main factors from other studies at a more abstract level.

SOCIAL CAPITAL: DIMENSIONS AND IMPLICATIONS

The concept of social capital originated from the idea that social relationships can be valuable resources. Adler and Kwon (2002) integrated different perspectives and defined social capital as 'the goodwill available to individuals or groups. Its source lies in the structure and content of the actor's social relations. Its effects flow from the information, influence, and solidarity it makes available to the actor' (p.23). Among three types of social governance mechanisms – market relations, hierarchical relations, and social relations – social capital primarily depends upon social relations, in which favours and gifts are exchanged under diffuse and tacit terms (Homans, 1974).

Because social capital's effects flow to individuals (Adler and Kwon, 2002), social capital is sometimes considered an individual attribute (Wasko and Faraj, 2005). At the individual level, social capital 'facilitates an actor's actions and reflects their access to network resources' (Wasko and Faraj 2005, p. 39). In other words, individuals can be said to possess social capital or to use it to achieve personal objectives. However, an individual cannot obtain the benefits of social capital without belonging to a larger social collective. Despite the effects of social capital on individuals, social capital can only be generated through social relations. In our analysis, we consider social capital to be a collective construct (Morgeson and Hofmann, 1999) that is constituted by individuals interacting (social relations) and which affects individuals. Thus, social capital can be described as an attribute of communities or other collectives, including industry networks and even nations. The social capital of a collectivity resides in the linkages among individuals or groups within the collectivity and in the cohesiveness that facilitates the pursuit of collective goals (Adler and Kwon, 2002). Indeed, our primary objective is to theorize about the relationship between social capital, as a collective construct, and the individual-level constructs of motivation and contribution.

Social capital is conceived along three dimensions, originally proposed by Nahapiet and Ghoshal (1998). The structural dimension of social capital concerns the connections among people. This dimension includes network ties, network configurations and network appropriability. Network ties are connections between members within a community that facilitate information and knowledge sharing and coordination of tasks. Network configuration is the pattern of ties such as structural holes, centralization and density. Different configurations of network ties can bring different benefits. Coleman (1988) argues that closure of network structure increases cohesiveness, and Burt (1992) argues that a sparse network aggregates resources for competitive action. OSS communities can benefit from both of these configurations. An OSS community is generally open to all so that it has potential to create a sparse network to aggregate and rally competency (Crowston and Scozzi, 2002). Meanwhile the team of core developers can enjoy the benefits of closure of the network. Network appropriability relates to the ease with which different types of relationships can be transferred within a network.

The relational dimension of social capital is characterized by high levels of trust, shared norms and mutual identification (Nahapiet and Ghoshal, 1998). Resilient trust and generalized trust play important roles in social capital creation and maintenance. Resilient trust is based on the experience with other parties and beliefs about their moral integrity without formal and contractual means, and it can survive through occasional transactions in which benefits and costs are not equalized. Generalized trust refers to the trust that can be generalized to all members within a collectivity. The norm of reciprocity is an important ingredient in social capital because the notion that 'I do this for you now and down the road somebody else will do the same for me' will promote sharing and collaboration. Identification refers to the phenomenon that people 'see themselves as one with another person or group of people' (Nahapiet and Ghoshal, 1998, p. 256). Identification with a community will align individual actions with collective processes and goals.

In an OSS community with a high level of relational social capital, individual developers would be expected trust each other, adhere to the norm of reciprocity and internalize their identity as community members. Thus, the ideology of collaboration is likely to influence individual contributions and project success (Stewart and Gosain, 2006). However, Gallivan (2001) raises doubts about the strength of trust in OSS communities and other virtual forms of organizing work. Based on a content analysis of case studies conducted on OSS communities, he concludes that implicit forms of social control operate so that communities do not have to depend exclusively on trust. For example, community members' contributions to an OSS project tend to be tested and evaluated rather than accepted on faith. Members are trusted if they perform capably, dependably and predictably but they are not trusted if they do not perform. Adler (2001) refers to this type of trust as reflective trust, which he contrasts with blind trust.

The cognitive dimension of social capital refers to shared representations, interpretations and systems of meaning among parties (Nahapiet and Ghoshal, 1998). It includes shared languages and shared narratives. Shared languages provide community members with the ability to communicate more effectively. A high level of cognitive social capital enables members within a community to have similar perceptions and interpretations of the same events. Shared narratives include myths, stories and metaphors that organizational members communicate to one another. Both shared languages and narratives increase the level of understanding among community members.

In an OSS community with a high level of cognitive social capital, shared languages enable users and developers to ask and answer questions in a way that can solve problems efficiently. Shared narrative also helps in creating, exchanging and preserving rich sets of meaning. This effect is expected to be similar to the effect of shared understanding in proprietary software development (Walz et al., 1993; Crowston and Kammerer, 1998).

As implied by the use of the label 'capital', social capital is assumed to bring benefits to individuals and organizations. This assumption has been validated in studies of career advancement (Lin, 1999; Seibert et al., 2001), organizational performance (Leana and Van Buren, 1999), and the ability of organizations to transform from private to public ownership (Fischer and Pollock, 2004). The concept of capital also implies a resource that can be depleted if social relationships deteriorate. For example, if networks of interaction are reconfigured to reduce social contact, members may draw from stocks of social capital without replenishing them (Schultze and Orlikowski, 2004). We expect that social capital will bring benefits to OSS communities and view it as an important resource affecting the outcomes of OSS projects. In the discussion below, we focus on three types of benefits identified by Adler and Kwon (2002): information, control and solidarity. We explain how each of these benefits helps to facilitate the process of OSS development and use.

The first direct benefit of social capital is information. Connections between people, trust and mutual understanding lying within social connections all make information sharing easier. Information and knowledge sharing is an essential activity in OSS communities because people within the community construct knowledge products collectively. Communication quality has been empirically associated with task completion in OSS development teams (Stewart and Gosain, 2006). Shared ideology regarding the value of collaboration has also been linked to communication quality (Stewart and Gosain, 2006). Sharing relevant information reduces the noise in messages and keeps a community focused on executing work more quickly. Timeliness of information sharing helps to speed up the bug reporting and repair processes.

Influence, control and power constitute the second benefit of social capital. People with high visibility and reputations tend to enjoy more of this benefit, but this benefit can also accrue to the collective level. In OSS communities, although work is not assigned according to a formal plan, project leaders assume important roles. Project leaders are either initiators of the project or people who make significant contributions to the project and establish their reputations in the community. As core developers, they decide what to include in the released versions of software and make other critical decisions affecting the community's destiny. Influence, control and power of the project team facilitates community acceptance of project decisions.

The third benefit of social capital is solidarity. Strong norms and beliefs, together with a high degree of network closure within the core group, encourage compliance with community rules and therefore reduce the need for formal controls. Shared norms can lower the monitoring costs and promote higher commitment. Solidarity enables community members to carry out collective tasks and reach collective goals. In a solidified OSS community, people try to align their own individual behaviours to collective actions and goals, producing an OSS product of high quality. They are more likely to follow community norms, and thus formal control and monitoring are needed less.

Given the positive effects of social capital on performance, we turn now to a theoretical model hypothesizing the relationships between social capital and individual contributions.

Research Propositions and Illustrations

To theorize the OSS phenomenon more completely, multiple levels of analysis can be taken into account (Klein et al., 1994; Morgeson and Hofmann, 1999). Every OSS community contains individual developers and users as well as a collective identity. In this chapter, we propose a cross-level model to explain the relationship between social capital in OSS communities and individual motivation and contribution (see Figure 5.1). Cross-level theories describe 'the relationship between independent and dependent variables at different levels' (Rousseau, 1985) and they are commonly used to describe the impact of group or organizational factors on individual behaviour and attitudes. Our model contains two levels: the community level and the individual level. Social capital is the community-level construct, and individual motivation and contribution are individual-level constructs.

We draw from published accounts of the Apache web server project and other sources to illustrate the propositions in the research model. This illustration should not be considered as a test of the model's propositions because the studies were not designed with such a test in mind. Although social capital is not a construct investigated by the previous research on Apache, the results

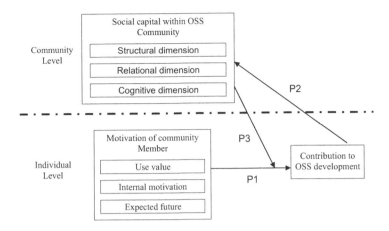

Figure 5.1   Theoretical model of social capital in OSS communities

of these studies refer to many of the same ideas encapsulated in our model. For this reason, we argue that the model is made more plausible, engendering confidence that the model is worthy of a more rigorous empirical test. We begin with a brief overview of the Apache web server project.

The Apache project is an OSS community with the objective to create and maintain an open-source HTTP (web) server. The Apache web server has become one the most popular web servers in use throughout the world. The project was initiated by a group of web masters in 1995 due to their dissatisfaction with the available web servers at that time. Geographically distributed volunteers in the Apache community used the internet to communicate, develop and distribute the server software and its documentation. The development of the Apache web server was not regulated by formal procedures. Volunteers chose to work on the parts they preferred rather than being given assignments. Within the Apache community, decision making was conducted by a group of leaders called the Apache Group, which was composed of people who had made significant contributions to the Apache project. The Apache Group used an email voting system to decide what contributed code to include in the final source code (Fielding, 1999).

MOTIVATIONS AND CONTRIBUTIONS OF OSS COMMUNITY MEMBERS

Our first proposition addresses the motives underlying volunteer contributions in OSS communities:

P1: Use value, intrinsic motivation, and expected future return motivate individual developers to contribute to OSS development.

P1 is consistent with prior research on the Apache web server. Hann et al. (2004) conducted a web-based survey of developers in three large Apache OSS projects to study the underlying dimensions of developer motivation and the relative importance of these dimensions. They conclude that five distinct factors of motivation are use-value, reputation, career concerns, normative reasons and recreation. Later analyses of the survey data reveal support for extrinsic motivations related to payment for contributions (Roberts et al., 2006). However, the later analysis also shows complex interactions between different motivations. For example, being paid to contribute has a negative effect on use-value motivation, while status motivations enhance intrinsic motivations (Roberts et al., 2006). Indeed, use-value motivations are associated with below-average contribution levels. These findings generally support the proposed relationship at the individual level, although our proposition does not incorporate the interactions among motivations.

P1 is also supported for Apache users, who offer free assistance to other users via Usenet postings. Lakhani and von Hippel (2003) offer substantial evidence of the motivation for user contributions to Apache Usenets. They conclude that '98 per cent of the effort invested by help providers was intrinsically rewarding to those providers via a particular feature of the task setting. That is, we found that the public posting of both questions and answers created a site that potential information providers wanted to visit and study in order to gain valuable information for themselves' (p. 940). Evidence of other expected future return motivations also appear to play a role, with 24 per cent of respondents agreeing with the statement 'I answer to enhance my career prospects,' and 28 per cent agreeing with the statement 'I want to enhance my reputation in OSS/Apache community' (Lakhani and von Hippel, 2003, p. 937). Thus, the voluntary contributions by individuals to the creation of a shared public good are motivated by intrinsic factors that return benefits to private contributors. P1 thus appears to find support from the Apache project.

P1 is also consistent with research on Linux user communities (Jin et al., 2006). Jin et al. find that participation in Linux User Groups (LUGs) helps users to solve their problems, establish and maintain social friendships and establish contacts that might convert to business opportunities. They also find that users are motivated by the desire to recruit new members into the Linux community. In addition, P1 is supported by related research in networked communities. For example, Wasko and Faraj (2005) find that motivations of online community members are based on desires for reputation and the enjoyment of helping others.

SOCIAL CAPITAL AS A BY-PRODUCT OF OSS DEVELOPMENT

Our second proposition addresses the production of social capital in OSS communities. In defining social capital, Adler and Kwon (2002) contrast community governance with both market and hierarchical governance. Whereas markets regulate activity with prices and hierarchies regulate with rules, community governance depends on social relations. In OSS communities, developers are not assigned to their jobs or bound by explicit employment contracts, and the OSS community provides the final product to users, not for return of economic profits but with the hope that users will contribute back to the community by reporting or fixing bugs. Gift culture and reciprocity norms are valued in the OSS community (Bergquist and Ljungberg, 2001). Thus:

> P2: The structural, relational and cognitive dimensions of social capital in the OSS community are created and maintained as a by-product of developers' participation in the community and their contributions to the project.

Adler and Kwon (2002) argue that three elements – opportunity, motivation, and ability – need to be present in social relations to form social capital. OSS communities contain each of these sources. First, the internet as a communication medium creates the opportunity for developers to connect with each other. Second, collective goals and belief in collective action – developing and using OSS software – motivate members to exchange knowledge both about source codes of specific software and about problems encountered in use. Third, members have the ability to conduct such exchanges because they come from similar backgrounds and share experiences and common language. Like other types of capital, social capital needs to be created and maintained. However, social capital cannot be created for the sole sake of creating it; it is always a by-product of other social activities and interactions.

The structural dimension of social capital is evident in the ties established as members work together and in the configuration network of a community's network. The structural dimension is often described in cases written about OSS projects because it is relatively easy to trace the network that governs the community. Like many other OSS projects, Apache operated with a team of core developers, 15 in number, who reviewed contributions offered by the wider community of developers and voted on the inclusion of any code changes (Mockus et al., 2000). This number remained stable over the first 10 years of the Apache project (Gonzalez-Barahona et al., 2004). Composition of the core group changed over time, however, given that all community members typically held other full-time jobs. The stable network structure of the Apache community was maintained as a valuable resource that channelled the contributions of members into released features and functions. This allowed the community to remain large while also converting member contributions into valuable outputs.

The relational dimension of social capital refers to the bonding between community members, indicating mutual trust among members who identify with community interests. This dimension is strengthened each time a member helps another member. Fielding, one of Apache's core developers, describes the sense of collective purpose in the project: 'We collaborate on producing and supporting the Apache server out of enlightened self-interest: by pooling our efforts, the resulting product is much more functional and robust than anything we could have produced alone' (Fielding, 1999, p. 42). Similar effects are reported in Lakhani and von Hippel's (2003) survey of Apache users, which shows reciprocity as the most frequent reason for helping others via Usenet postings.

The cognitive dimension of social capital is strengthened as developers and users communicate in a common language, thus increasing the amount of information that can be conveyed. This by-product of individual development contributions has not been studied directly for the Apache project, but it seems almost axiomatic that high levels of communication would require, and reproduce, the use of a common language. As Walz et al. (1993) and Crowston and Kammerer (1998) show, common ground for communication is also essential in traditional software development efforts.

EFFECTS OF SOCIAL CAPITAL ON INDIVIDUAL MOTIVATION AND CONTRIBUTION

The third proposition addresses the effects of social capital on individual motivation and contribution:

*P3: Social capital within an OSS community has a positive impact on
the relationship between individual developers' motivation levels and
their contribution levels.*

This relationship is the most complex one in the model: a cross-level moderating impact of social capital upon the relationship between individual motivations and individual contributions. Where community-level social capital is high, we expect a stronger relationship between individual motivation and contributions. Social capital is one of the incentives that helps to reconcile the inherent conflict between personal and community interests (Kollock and Smith, 1996). In an OSS community with a low level of social capital, motivations to contribute are expected to have a weaker relationship with actual contributions because members will not feel that their participation in the community and contribution to the project are rewarding. Therefore, they are less encouraged to contribute intensively on the project.

These moderating effects are expected to hold true for each of the three types of motivations discussed earlier. First, community-level social capital rewards developers with 'use value' motivations. Developers with use value motivations care the most about the quality of the software developed in an OSS community. Where social capital is high, use value motivation is more strongly linked to individual contributions because both individual and collective benefits are more likely to occur.

Second, community-level social capital strengthens the relationship between 'intrinsic motivation' and individual contributions. Developers with intrinsic motivation contribute to OSS projects because they see programming tasks as learning or recreation. In communities with a high level of social capital, connections between persons, trust and mutual identification, and common cognitive understanding establish an environment in which members can fulfil their intrinsic motives, making work on the project enjoyable and educational. In communities with low social capital, intrinsically motivated developers would be more frustrated by having to learn on their own rather than drawing from the experiences of fellow members.

Third, community-level social capital rewards developers who are motivated by expected future returns. People expecting future returns want to improve their programming skills and/or increase their reputations with their work on the OSS project. In communities with high levels of social capital, members are more likely to share information about programming knowledge and skills while bestowing reputations on those who contribute most.

Understandably, P3 is not a relationship that the case studies and surveys on Apache (or any other OSS project) have addressed directly. However, P3 is consistent with summary statements about the importance of community support on developer and user efforts. For example, in discussing the skills needed for OSS developers to contribute effectively to Apache, Yan et al. (2005) conclude: 'Such skills include the ability to participate in the open-source community activities such as news groups and discussion forums. Developers are more productive when they learn to embrace the open-source culture' (p. 424). Not only does this statement support our proposition about effects of individual contributions on increasing social capital (P2), but also the positive influence of social capital on the relationship between motivations and individual contributions. Apache is an example of how a supportive community, rich in social capital, can provide the environment (or culture) in which individuals are most likely to see their motivations lead to productive contributions. By contrast, less supportive communities might actually stifle individual motivations, thereby reducing actual contributions and their resulting benefits to the individual and the community.

Shah (2006) lends indirect support for P3 in her comparative study of 'open' and 'gated' OSS development communities. In an open community, a project's licensing terms generally allow anyone to download, use, modify and distribute software code (Shah, 2006, p. 1002). In a gated OSS community, by contrast, downloading, use and modification of code are restricted to those who agree to a licence with a corporate sponsor, who legally owns the code and reserves the right to select modifications from those contributed. In gated communities, sponsors collect royalties from commercial uses of the software. Shah finds that governance structure moderates the relationship between motivation and contribution. In the open community, volunteers (many described as hobbyists) contribute as a form of reciprocity to the community. Contributions are thus affected by the relational social capital in the community. By contrast, the gated community is one with less social capital because it operates on different governance principles. As Shah concludes, 'the same individual might act differently and be driven by different motives in different contexts' (p. 1010). Although social capital is not studied directly, differences in community governance clearly affect the relationships between motivations to contribute and the degree of contribution.

Implications for Research and Practice

In this chapter, we propose a cross-level model to explain the role of social capital in OSS communities. Like many social phenomena, OSS communities are inherently multi-level phenomena involving both collective and individual resources. We believe it is important to study the OSS phenomenon through the lens of a model that focuses on the relationships between constructs at different levels. The model examines relationships across levels of analysis, thereby providing a more comprehensive view of the OSS community and OSS development and use.

RESEARCH IMPLICATIONS

Several research implications are worth noting. First, the model offers a novel conceptualization of the relationship between community and individual characteristics. It reinforces the interest in reasons why individuals contribute their valuable personal resources in the production of public goods, which has been the subject of so many studies. Moreover, the model offers insight into the moderating effect of community characteristics on individual decisions to devote time and effort to OSS projects. By using the concept of social capital at the community level, we hope to capture theoretically a major influence on the relationships operating at the level of individual contributors to OSS projects. By emphasizing the community's influence on individuals, we overcome the more limited view in previous research. We propose that social capital moderates the relationship between individual motivation and contributions. In this relationship, the importance of social capital as a community resource becomes apparent, as it reinforces the motivation to contribute. We encourage future research to investigate community-level influences more deeply.

Second, little attention has been paid to the process of building community social capital. We propose that social capital accumulates as a by-product of individual contributions to the community. However, future research should examine more carefully how such good will accumulates as a community resource. Aside from accepted principles such as reciprocity and social obligation, less is known about the way that individuals understand the contributions received from others in the community and the expectations that follow. We understand why individuals contribute to the creation of public goods, but we know less about their subsequent expectations in terms of community benefit. It would be naïve to assume that individuals would contribute altruistically without some assurance that their efforts would be rewarded at some level. Developers in the centre of a community may realize more benefits from social capital than peripheral members, even though social capital is theoretically a community resource. For example, core developers in large successful OSS projects may convert social capital into personal economic capital by entering the commercial software industry (von Hippel and von Krogh, 2003). This private benefit may not accrue to all members of the community.

These considerations raise questions about the durability or sustainability of community governance. As OSS and other communities mature, community structure and the allocation of benefits is likely to change, even within sub-modules of OSS projects. An important research stream for the future, therefore, involves examination of how community structures and individual motivations will affect future commitments to contribute. As commercial interests exercise more influence in OSS communities, the effect of community social capital on individual contributors may change drastically.

These concerns suggest that, in subsequent iterations, our model could be transformed to capture dynamic cross-level influences. Such a transformation might require a departure from the static, variance form of modelling to a more dynamic, process model (Mohr, 1982). For example, the three propositions could be formulated as a cycle of mutually reinforcing activities or events in which individual motivations and their contributions to OSS development generate social capital as by-product, which in turn strengthens the relationship between motivation and contribution. Such positive cycles are difficult to represent in variance models where dynamic implications are generally masked by static relationships. Although converting the model's form is beyond our present purpose, a process model would stimulate new research questions pertaining to the evolution and progression of OSS communities. In particular, a process model could address questions relevant to the role that social capital plays in motivating individuals to contribute to the creation of public goods. In addition, where commercial interests intervene in community-led efforts, we might see an erosion of social capital and a corresponding reduction in the strength of individual motivations to contribute.

PRACTICAL IMPLICATIONS

If validated empirically, our model has significant practical implications. The model explains that community-level social capital moderates the relationship between individuals' motivation and their contributions to the community.

This insight has significant implications for OSS community leaders, who could strive to invest in social capital within their communities. OSS participants (including users and developers) should also understand the importance of community-level social capital and contribute toward building it. Because social capital is a by-product of individual contributions to OSS software projects and participation in user communities, all members can add to the investment in social capital.

Outsiders may also gain insights from the model. Commercial software companies may adopt aspects of the OSS community model to establish processes for software development and user support. Recent reports suggest that commercial software companies have experimented with the OSS community model to improve the process of building software (Mockus and Herbsleb, 2002; Henkel, 2004). The theoretical insights provided in our model can also apply to this situation.

Given these potential implications, the question remains: how can OSS communities foster greater investments in social capital? Rather than letting social capital passively accumulate as a by-product of individual contributions, as the model suggests, there may be more direct ways for leaders and members to build and maintain this vital community resource. The literature on social capital provides some possible answers. First, advocates of social capital advise that members of a community be brought together in settings where they can meet face to face (Prusak and Cohen, 2001). While sensible in principle, this advice is difficult to implement in OSS projects, where the vast majority of communication is conducted through electronic media. Such virtuality 'erodes relationships...which is why managers must learn to invest in social capital' (Prusak and Cohen, 2001, p. 88).

Despite the extreme virtuality of OSS communities, both developers and users do meet face to face on a somewhat regular basis in different forums. Linux World Conference and other major conferences are convened so that members of the community can hear speeches from core developers and meet in smaller groups to discuss specific topics. Linux is also supported by a number of Linux User Groups, which hold monthly regional meetings in Silicon Valley and other centres where software cultures thrive (Jin et al., 2006). Crowston et al. (2005) note the lack of studies on the role of face-to-face interaction among OSS developers. They report a study of OSS developers working in teams that occasionally met face to face at several conferences, including ApacheCom.

Their observations suggest that such meetings are important to develop social ties between developers, many of whom were meeting for the first time.

In addition to face-to-face meetings, members of OSS communities can use electronic media to expand communication topics beyond technical problem solving. Internet communication can be enhanced by supporting social activities conducted online. The purpose of these activities is to strengthen motivation by sharing cultural values and assumptions. As with any culture, folklore can develop involving stories about heroes (e.g., Eric Raymond, Linus Torvalds) and celebrating the difference between OSS and commercial software values.

Finally, maintaining a clear social structure for OSS communities allows members to build social capital because the structure allows more talented members to progress from peripheral positions (e.g., bug reporter) to more central positions, perhaps eventually becoming core developers (Ye and Agarwal, 2003). Although tangible rewards are not distributed, high-performing members are rewarded in effect by promotion within the network structure. By allowing members at the periphery to participate legitimately (Lave and Wenger, 1991), communities foster learning through practice and strengthen the bonds between members. Because OSS communities are communities that produce actual goods in the form of software, member ability is important and recognizable.

Conclusion

In this chapter, we propose a cross-level model to explain the role of social capital in OSS communities. We discuss how community-level social capital can be created and maintained as a by-product of ongoing activities within an OSS community. Community-level social capital, as a valuable resource shared by community members, is assumed to provide direct information, control, and solidarity benefits to the OSS community as a whole, facilitating the software development process. Community-level social capital works as a positive reinforcement for developers' contributions. In an OSS community with a high level of social capital, developers will be more encouraged to make contributions.

Our argument is not free of limitations. First, we have not discussed the potential negative impact of social capital. As with any other form of capital, investment and efforts are necessary to create and maintain social capital.

Thus, it may be that benefits do not outweigh the investment. Second, social capital also could make OSS communities more insular. For example, cohesion resulting from high levels of relational social capital could create a barrier for new members to join, and closure in small groups could split the community and jeopardize community-wide solidarity. Finally, the model is limited by a lack of empirical validation. Subsequent testing and refinement of the model are thus needed.

Despite these limitations, the proposed model has potential to contribute to both research and practice. In terms of research, it advances our understanding of the relationship between community-level social capital and individual-level motivations and contributions in OSS communities. The model can also be generalized to other communities adopting the private-collective model of innovation creation (e.g., Jeppesen and Frederiksen, 2006). In terms of practice, the model helps OSS community leaders, as well as commercial software producers who intend to incorporate OSS elements into software development, to realize the important role of social capital. Leaders or project managers should strive to create a community environment with a high level social capital, which will keep developers motivated to produce high-quality software.

References

Adler, P.S. (2001). Market, Hierarchy, and Trust: The Knowledge Economy and the Future of Capitalism. *Organization Science* 12(2): 215–34.

Adler, P.S. and S.-W. Kwon (2002). Social Capital: Prospects for a New Concept. *Academy of Management Review* 27(1): 17–40.

Bergquist, M. and J. Ljungberg (2001). The Power of Gifts: Organizing Social Relationships in Open Source Communities. *Information Systems Journal* 11: 305–20.

Burt, R.S. (1992). *Structural Holes: The Social Structure of Competition.* Cambridge, MA: Harvard University Press.

Coleman, J.S. (1988). Social Capital in the Creation of Human Capital. *American Journal of Sociology*, S95–S120.

Crowston, K., J. Howison, C. Masango and U.Y. Eseryel (2005). *Face-to-face Interactions in Self-organizing Distributed Teams.* OCIS division, Academy of Management Conference.

Crowston, K. and E. Kammerer (1998). Coordination and Collective Mind in Software Requirements Development. *IBM Systems Journal* 37(2): 227–45.

Crowston, K. and B. Scozzi (2002). Open Source Software Projects as Virtual Organisations: Competency Rallying for Software Development. Software Engineering, IEE Proceedings.

Dinh-Trong, T.T. and J.M. Bieman (2005). The FreeBSD Project: A Replication Case Study of Open Source Development. *IEEE Transactions on Software Engineering* 31(6): 481–94.

Dotzler, A. (2003). Getting Involved with Mozilla: The People, the Tools, the Process. *L. U. G. O.* Davis, CA: Mozilla.org.

Fielding, R.T. (1999). Shared Leadership in the Apache Project. *Communications of ACM* 42(4): 42–3.

Fischer, H.M. and T.G. Pollock (2004). Effects of Social Capital and Power on Surviving Transformational Change: The Case of Internal Public Offerings. *Academy of Management Journal* 47: 463–81.

Fitzgerald, B. and T. Kenny (2004). Developing an Information Systems Infrastructure with Open Source Software. *IEEE Software* 21(1): 50–55.

Franke, N. and E. von Hippel (2003). Satisfying Heterogeneous User Needs via Innovation Toolkits: The Case of Apache Security Software. *Research Policy* 32(7): 1199–215.

Gallivan, M.J. (2001). Striking a Balance Between Trust and Control in a Virtual Organization: A Content Analysis of Open Source Software Case Studies. *Information Systems Journal* 11: 277–304.

Gonzalez-Barahona, J.M., L. Lopez-Fernandez and G. Robles (2004). *Community Structure of Modules in the Apache Project*. Proceedings of the 4th Workshop on Open Source Software Engineering, Edinburgh, Scotland, UK.

Hann, I.-H., J. Roberts and S.A. Slaughter (2004). *Why Developers Participate in Open Source Software Projects: An Empirical Investigation*. Twenty-Fifth International Conference on Information Systems, Washington, D.C.

Hann, I.-H., J. Roberts, S.A. Slaughter and R. Fielding (2003). *Economic Incentives for Participating in Open Source Software Projects*. Twenty-Third International Conference on Information Systems.

Hars, A. and S. Ou (2000). Why is Open Source Software Viable? – A Study of Intrinsic Motivation, Personal Needs, and Future Returns. *Americas Conference of Information Systems*: 486–90.

Henkel, J. (2004). Open Source Software from Commercial Firms – Tools, Complements, and Collective Invention. *Zeitschrift Für Betriebswirtschaft, Supplement* 4: 1–23.

Homans, G.C. (1974). *Social Behavior: Its Elementary Forms*. New York: Harcourt Brace Jovanovich.

Ireland, R.D., M.A. Hitt and D. Vaidyanath (2002). Alliance Management as a Source of Competitive Advantage. *Journal of Management* 28(3): 413–46.

Jeppesen, L. B. and L. Frederiksen (2006). Why Do Users Contribute to Firm-Hosted User Communities? The Case of Computer-Controlled Music Instruments. *Organization Science* 17(1): 45–63.

Jin, L., D. Robey and M.-C. Boudreau (2006). Exploring the Hybrid Community: Intertwining Virtual and Physical Representations of Linux User Communities. *Proceedings of the Administrative Science Association of Canada*, Banff, Canada, June 4–6.

Jin, L., D. Robey and M.-C. Boudreau (2007). Beyond Development: A Research Agenda for Investigating Open Source Software User Communities. *Information Resources Management Journal*, 20(1): 68–80.

Klein, K.J., F. Dansereau and R.J. Hall (1994). Levels Issues in Theory Development, Data Collection, and Analysis. *Academy of Management Review* 19: 195–229.

Kollock, P. and M. Smith (1996). Managing the Virtual Commons: Cooperation and Conflict in Computer Communities, in S.C. Herring (ed.) *Computer-Mediated Communications: Linguistic, Social and Cross-Cultural Perspectives*. Philadelphia: John Benjamins.

Lakhani, K.R. and E. von Hippel (2003). How Open Source Software Works: 'Free' User-to-user Assistance. *Research Policy* 32(6): 923–43.

Lakhani, K.R., B. Wolf, J. Bates and C. Dibona (2002). *The Boston Consulting Group Hacker Survey*. Boston Consulting Group and Open Source Developers Network, July 24, 2002. http://ftp3.au.freebsd.org/pub/linux.conf.au/2003/papers/Hemos/Hemos.pdf, last accessed October 19, 2010.

Lave, J. and E. Wenger (1991). *Situated Learning: Legitimate Peripheral Participation*. Cambridge: Cambridge University Press.

Leana, C. and H.J. Van Buren III (1999). Organizational Social Capital and Employment Practices. *Academy of Management Review* 24(3): 538–55.

Lin, N. (1999). Social Networks and Status Attainment. *Annual Review of Sociology* 25: 467–87.

Mockus, A., R.T. Fielding and J. Herbsleb (2000). A Case Study of Open Software Development: The Apache Server. Proceedings of 22nd International Conference of Software Engineering, Limerick, Ireland June 5–7: 263–72.

Mockus, A. and J.D. Herbsleb (2002). Why Not Improve Coordination in Distributed Software Development by Stealing Good Ideas from Open Source? International Conference on Software Engineering (ICSE 2002), Orlando, FL, USA: 35–7, May 2002.

Mohr, L. (1982). *Explaining Organizational Behavior*. San Francisco, Jossey-Bass.

Morgeson, F.P. and D.A. Hofmann (1999). The Structure and Function of Collective Constructs: Implications for Multilevel Research and Theory Development. *Academy of Management Review* 24: 249–65.

Nahapiet, J. and S. Ghoshal (1998). Social Capital, Intellectual Capital, and the Organizational Advantage. *Academy of Management Review* 23(2): 242–66.

Prusak, L. and D. Cohen (2001). How to Invest in Social Capital. *Harvard Business Review* 79(6): 86–93.

Raymond, E.S. (1999). *The Cathedral and the Bazaar: Musings on Linux and Open Source by an Accidental Revolutionary*. Sebastopol, CA: O'Reilly and Associates.

Roberts, J.A., I.-H. Hann and S.A. Slaughter (2006). Understanding the Motivations, Participation, and Performance of Open Source Software Developers: A Longitudinal Study of the Apache Projects. *Management Science* 52(7): 984–99.

Rousseau, D.M. (1985). Issues of Level in Organizational Research: Multi-level and Cross-level Perspectives. *Research in Organizational Behavior* 7: 1–37.

Schultze, U. and W.J. Orlikowski (2004). A Practice Perspective on Technology-Mediated Network Relations: The Use of Internet-Based Self-Serve Technologies. *Information Systems Research* 15(1): 87–106.

Seibert, S.E., M.L. Kraimer and R.C. Liden (2001). A Social Capital Theory of Career Success. *Academy of Management Journal* 44(2): 219–37.

Shah, S.K. (2006). Motivation, Governance, and the Viability of Hybrid Forms in Open Source Software Development. *Management Science* 52(7): 1000–1014.

Stewart, K.J. and S. Gosain (2006). The Moderating Role of Development Stage in Free/Open Source Software Project Performance. *Software Process: Improvement and Practice* 11(2): 177–91.

Von Hippel, E. and G. von Krogh (2003). Open Source Software and the Private-collective Innovation Model: Issues for Organization Science. *Organization Science* 14(2): 209–23.

Walz, D.B., J.J. Elam and B. Curtis (1993). Inside a Software Design Team: Knowledge Acquisition, Sharing, and Integration. *Communications of the ACM* 36(10): 63–77.

Wasko, M.M. and S. Faraj (2005). Why Should I Care? Examining Social Capital and Knowledge Contribution in Electronic Networks of Practice. *MIS Quarterly* 29(1): 35–57.

Yan, N., D. Leip and K. Gupta (2005). The Use of Open-source Software in the IBM Corporate Portal. *IBM Systems Journal* 44(2): 419–25.

Ye, F. and R. Agarwal (2003). Strategic Information Technology Partnerships in Outsourcing as a Distinctive Source of Information Technology Value: A Social Capital Perspective. 24th International Conference on Information Systems. *ICIS 2003 Proceedings*. Paper 26. http://aisel.aisnet.org/icis2003/26.

Ye, Y. and K. Kishida (2003). Toward an Understanding of the Motivation of
    Open Source Developers. Proceedings of the 25th International Conference
    on Software Engineering, Portland, OR, USA, 419–29.

6

How Far Do Informal Credits in Free Software Go?

Matthias Bärwolff

Introduction

Even the most casual look at the state of free software reveals its almost mainstream acceptance both as an input to production as well as a means of producing software in the first place. Analyses have put the commercial value created through free software projects worldwide at several billion dollars per year.[1] This value may to a large extent end up with the actual consumers of free software; however, a certain margin is bound to be left with those producing and marketing the software. After all, why would commercial entities such as RedHat and IBM become involved with free software if there was no benefit from doing so? Clearly, there are ways to benefit from one's involvement with free software in plain money terms (Bärwolff 2006).

It should also be noted that, despite the lack of participants' explicit contractual commitments to free software projects, economically speaking, such projects are firms just like any other incorporated firm (Iacobucci and Triantis 2007). Thus, in theory, participants may be held accountable to standard commercial duty of care even if their contributions are neither remunerated nor paid for by the actual consumer.

The above considerations about its institutional 'normality' notwithstanding, free software has at least one prominent characteristic rendering it distinct from

---

1   Software market analysts regularly put the commercial value of Linux, one of the most high-profile free software projects, at several billion dollars (see e. g. IDC 2004). Ghosh et al. (2006) put the annual value created by the major free software projects at €800 million with commercial entities such as SUN, IBM and RedHat accounting for more than half of all contributions.

the received economic categories market and firm. It is the lack of excludability in free software by virtue of its liberal licensing scheme that forms its institutional essence and the principal legal means of enforcing the prime objective of free software – the perpetual freedom of the software's source code (Gehring 2005). Unfettered access to the software is not discriminated by means other than the recipient's willingness to abide by licensing terms stipulating that they must relicense any derivative work that they redistribute under the very same free licence. The resulting governance structure may be considered an economic mode that is neither firm nor market (Demil and Lecocq 2006).

The question arises as to what incentivises individuals and firms to contribute their scarce resources to what amounts to a free software commons. Ordinarily, public goods will be underprovided by markets due to the divergence of public and private utility (Stiglitz 1999). And yet, we have seen above that there are contexts in which customers pay developers of free software despite its curious characteristic of effectively free, and thus generally available free of charge. Direct transactions involving money exchange do not always work, however; and a number of explanations have been put forward to account for those 'transactions' in which no exchange of money is involved. Those range from considerations of mere 'fun' (Osterloh et al. 2002) to the signalling of one's skills to potential employers or customers (Lerner and Tirole 2002). These motivations do, indeed, explain much of the efforts going into free software development. The crucial point is not only that these motivations incentivise people to direct efforts into working at free software better than money can do, but that in software development these motivations often make for a superior resource allocation mechanism than ordinary money-incentivised ones.

Yet, as so often in life, things come at a cost which needs to be balanced with the benefits. In the case of free software those costs are primarily the limited scope of informal credit redemption as we shall see later in this chapter. The consequence of this qualifying consideration is that there is a trade-off to be made in the devising of an appropriate institutional framework for free software development. Managers rushing to copy successful attempts at mobilising people to work in a free software project must always think about the returns that are available to those they are aiming to recruit. Similarly, economic policies aiming at supporting free software industries have to take the broader considerations of credits and their redemption into due consideration.

In this chapter we work towards a notion of credits beyond money and how it applies to the development of free software, both as an enabling and as a limiting factor. The chapter's main contribution is introduction of the notion of credits as a means of commerce and asset allocation in general to the reality of free software. This view provides a level of abstraction that turns out to be very helpful in modelling many of the phenomena observed in free software projects and their interrelation with society at large.

The chapter proceeds as follows. First, we will consider the general nature of credits in commerce and the inevitable incompleteness of contracts over software due to the structural complexity of software. This leads us to the dilemma between private and public interests regarding the control over one's efforts in the development of software by means of restricting its use and withholding its source code. Finally, we will elaborate on the structure of informal contracts and credits in free software, and, last, we consider the limitations to their application.

Informal Credits and Incomplete Contracts

The importance of the institution of credit in general for the economic development of society cannot be overstated. It is the foundation of any meaningful commerce amongst individuals and groups of people in a society, as it allows the reciprocation of services and goods in a delayed manner. Consequently, opening up a much wider horizon of transactions than would be possible in an idealised barter economy (Innes 1914).

Today, we often tend to reduce the notion of credit to central bank issued and state backed money, possibly extended to its closer relatives that may be denoted in pecuniary terms. It is, indeed, hard to see why anyone would *not* prefer to realise the gains from trade their efforts give rise to in the intermediate shape of money. However, credits in social interactions have forever been taking a host of shapes ranging from tacit agreement amongst individuals on delayed reciprocation, to such understandings made in public involving the threat of punishment by third parties in case of failure to reciprocate, to the bank-issued and state-controlled money so prominent in modern-day transactions. Money is but one form of credit, and credit as a general means of accounting for debts and according credits is probably as old as mankind itself (Henry 2004; Hudson 2004). Most if not all native societies had developed dedicated institutions of property rights and means of credits to sustain their economies (Malinowski 1922).

Any system of credit accounting entails costs whose magnitude depends on the specifics regarding the interplay of law and norms, the economic environment and the nature of the assets to be transferred (Coase 1937). While money has arguably been the most easily transferable and universal form of credit throughout the history of capitalism (Ingham 2004) it is important to realise that it need not always be the most efficient means of credit. There have always been areas in society where money credits play little to no role precisely because they entail higher transaction costs than other more informal means of credits. Particularly in economic systems where trust and reciprocity are deeply entrenched, a system of tacit accounting economises on the transaction costs inevitably associated with the maintenance of a monetary system. Means of reciprocity and its enforcement depend not on the particular form of credits used, but the broader institutional setting (Bowles 2004; Diekmann 2004; Bolton and Ockenfels 2000; Falk and Fischbacher 2000).

Informal accounting practices typically lack the very formality required to feasibly enforce agreements in a court of law. However, the same often goes for written contracts subject to the full force of contract law. Whenever the assets to a transaction are difficult to specify, knowledge and rationality of the participants are bounded, and the contingencies of a transaction may not be fully captured in all detail, we are inevitably left with incomplete contracts (Grossman and Hart 1986; Hart and Moore 1988). Thus incomplete contracts along with more or less informal accounting for credits are actually the rule rather than the exception. To quote Durkheim (1893): 'Not everything in the contract is contractual [...] the contract is not sufficient in itself but possible only thanks to a regulation of the contract, which is social in origin' (p. 189 and p. 193). Complete contracts may, in fact, be less efficient and more costly than incomplete contracts, as in favourable social conditions incomplete contracts often induce the exertion of social norms to make up for the incompleteness (Fehr and Gächter 2000). This is true even in cases where it was perfectly feasible to write a more complete contract. In 'frequently repeated, multifaceted, face-to-face situations' often found in 'groupings referred to as communities' (Bowles 2004, p. 258) it is very common to not even try and write complete contracts and invest in monitoring performance but to count on social institutions to help enforce compliance with an agreement. Many real-world transactions are thus deliberately extended 'beyond the shadow of law' (Ellickson 1991).

Complexity, Software Value, and Free Software

With even moderately complex software, the problems of bounded rationality and contractual complexity discussed earlier are particularly pronounced. Considering the myriad interdependencies of different software modules on a typical computer system, it is plain to see that complete contracts over software are elusive if not impossible to conclude (Bessen 2005, p. 2). Furthermore, the problem of complexity applies both to the production and the distribution or sale of software. It is hard for users to specify their demand, it is hard for a manager to monitor the work efforts of programmers, in fact it is hard for anyone even to judge the state, the progress and the quality of a software project (Rosenberg 2007). It is, thus, little wonder that a substantial part of software development is not being conducted in competitive market contexts governed solely by price signals. Most software today is either subject to monopolist practices or is being developed and maintained in-house.[2]

The inevitable contractual incompleteness entails costs which have to be allocated between the parties involved in the transactions over software. Generally, these costs are being shifted to the consumer by means of warranty disclaimers in the licensing terms. When combined with the common practice of withholding the source code to software the customer is left with a detriment sufficient to create an 'adversarial relationship' with the vendor (Assay 2005). We may call this effect the value-control dilemma. The source code of a software makes it more valuable to a user, and even more so under a liberal free software licence.[3] Yet this shifts control over the software to the user which in turn makes it harder for a producer to maximise his surplus. Maximising the aggregate value of a software inevitably entails a loss of control and, thus, direct profit opportunity by the producer. Hence a rational producer will choose to remain at an 'adversarial relationship' with his customers, withholding the source code and keeping tight control over the software, in particular when he commands a monopoly market with little competition.

---

2   In fact the anti-competitive characteristics of the 'information good' software often blamed for this situation, namely lock-in and network effects (Shapiro and Varian 1999), may actually be traced back to the complexity of software, for ultimately, the inefficiencies in the software market are a consequence of the inevitable incompleteness of contracts following from the complexity of software.

3   Note that software written in higher level languages such as Python or Java is often distributed in its source code, for such programs are typically being interpreted in their original form, not in a compiled machine code. However, proprietary licences and support contracts often prohibit any modification of the code on the part of the user. See also footnote 4 and the accompanying text for the costs from mastering the complexity of code even in its source form.

The complexity of software has a further consequence affecting its transferability in a social system and its appropriation. Even in the presence of source code, a user will not easily be able to capture full control over a software. To understand and wholly appropriate a software artefact is a costly endeavour that may in the case of even moderately complex software systems well be beyond the capabilities of a single mind.[4] The problem is aggravated with poor software design, code quality and documentation. It is thus often easier to rewrite software from scratch than to rely on existing code.[5]

Whilst complexity is a structural feature of software, several solutions have been proposed to cope with it (Brooks Jr. 1995; Rosenberg 2007). Bessen (2005) has proposed three principal optimisation strategies to deal with the issue of complexity:

1.   Offer a package with a wide range of functionalities accounting for as many contingencies as possible, thus satisfying a large number of possible needs on the demand side.

2.   Shift part of the solution building to the consumer by offering modules with limited functionalities (and thus contingencies) well enough specified to interface with other modules.

3.   Contribute code to a free software commons, waiving the exclusive ownership of one's investments and thus avoiding the resulting contractual hassles. The larger the existing commons, the more attractive this solution will be.

Whilst the former two solutions reduce complexity by attempting to contain the contractual contingencies, the latter additionally overcomes the 'adversarial relationship' between vendors and users simply because there are no more vendors. Economides and Katsamakas (2005) argue similarly that application providers for platforms may be seen as 'indirect' users of such software and will thus generally not only favour the platform for their application to be free software but also have a consequent incentive to contribute to such a platform as it makes the overall package of the platform plus its differentiating applications more attractive to prospective users. Such contributions are also viable because

---

4   Often not even the producer of a software masters the complexity of his product in its entirety. The due knowledge is typically of tacit and uncodified nature, dispersed through an organisation at best, and beyond central planning and control.

5   For an interesting account of the Mozilla rewrite of the Netscape browser see, e.g., Bauer and Pizka (2003).

there are generally no significant opportunity costs (in the shape of profits forgone) for backing a free software platform further down the software stack, apart from the efforts incurred in contributing.[6]

A related argument is that of 'user innovation' put forward by von Hippel (2005) which is broader in scope and may be applied not only to software but to any goods that lend themselves to actively involving the users in their shaping. Von Hippel's model builds on the premise that precise information about user demand cannot be perfectly communicated to the supply side due to the transaction costs involved. Thus it is in some instances more efficient for users, particularly 'lead users' to amend an existing product according to their needs by themselves and freely reveal their innovation to others.[7]

The limitation to handing over control and responsibility is that at least some users will have to contribute themselves or invest in due contributions to the solution of his problem. Bessen thus limits the scope of his considerations to 'more complex, "geekier" applications' (p. 4) where users tend to be producers, too. The incentive puzzle becomes more pronounced when producers and users are more disparate, and efforts put into free software are not merely in-house improvements whose publication is a mandatory consequence of the respective free software licence.[8] In this case the benefits from the involvement in free software projects do not as easily accrue to a contributor. The value-control dilemma mentioned above would only be alleviated if there were ways for a producer to recoup his investments by means other than the generation of conventional credits in money terms. The following section will address the question under which circumstances a producer will sensibly choose the

---

6   See, e.g., the high-profile involvement of IBM in Linux, or that of SAP in the free software database management system MaxDB (Smith 2006, p. 85).

7   Note, however, that the approach of 'user innovation' may be subsumed under general microeconomic theory when users that innovate choose to become producers in their own rights, something that frequently happens (Shah and Tripsas 2004; Tripsas 2006). Note, also, that contributing even small modifications to a software – made out of private necessities – to a commons confers benefits to third parties which are not generally paid for in pecuniary terms. This would only be sensible if the costs saved by building one's particular solution upon an existing free software exceed those of the profits foregone from creating and licensing a proprietary solution to third-party beneficiaries. The due contribution to a commons may in such instances be modelled as an unpaid externality resulting from the transaction costs foreclosing market transactions over the improvements.

8   Note that modifications to a free software need only be published when the software is further distributed. Modifications that remain in-house or are subject to BSD (Berkeley Software Distribution) or BSD-like licensing terms need not be contributed back to the upstream project. However, there is some incentive to do so in order not to be cut off from any newer versions of the software modified by effectively having created a fork that would not automatically or easily inherit any modifications in the upstream project.

free software strategy, and the way credits are generated and redeemed in the context of free software.

Informal Credits in Free Software

The overall merit of a particular organisation of efforts is one thing, getting people to put in their efforts in the first place or incumbents to waive their positions is an entirely different matter. We have in the preceding section briefly considered externalities from privately motivated modifications to free software as one explanation for contributions.[9] Yet we have also noted that people will generally try to internalise such externalities if the costs of doing so do not exceed the benefits. The crucial question is, then, how to ameliorate the value-control dilemma faced by producers such that they can realise a significant enough part of the value added by dispensing with tight control so as to incentivise their very act of doing so.

The classic approach to reconcile divergent private and public ends is that of imposing taxes or affording subsidies to make up for the differences between the two (Pigou 1932). Along those lines have proposed alternative compensation systems to create revenues for free software contributors from levies or taxes (Fleissner 2006).[10] However, this approach suffers from equally classic shortcomings due to the costs involved in gathering the information needed to sustain such interventions without creating new divergences between social and private interests (Coase 1960; Hayek 1945).

It is useful to look at how benefits from one's efforts are typically realised in the decentralised environment that our society creates. Generally three vital things are involved:

- a means of evaluating the merit of individual contributions

- accounting for merits through appropriate credits

- the redemption of those credits for contributions of others.

---

9   See footnote 7 and accompanying text.
10 The principal logic follows that of proposals of alternative compensation systems in the field of content such as music and texts which would make futile the current prohibitions so prominent in the existing copyright regime. Such systems are already in place to a certain degree.

Ordinarily, from a market's perspective the merit of one's contribution is taken to simply follow directly from the price in money terms others are willing to pay for it. Those payments then take the form of money which is a credit that may then be redeemed elsewhere, mostly for goods that are traded in free markets (Innes 1914). In a firm, the price mechanism is absent but individual contributions will be monitored to a certain degree, and payment is made accordingly (Coase 1937), again, mostly by means of money.[11]

Generally, due to the absence of prices and exclusive ownerships, the credit model found in markets and firms cannot be applied to free software. However, there is one notable exception. As long as a creator of a software has not distributed it to anyone it is still scarce. It may thus be at least for one time licensed for a fee that will reflect its value to the licensee. From this point on competition on the supply side will swiftly bring the price of the software to zero reflecting the unlimited availability. Boldrin and Levine (2002) have argued that in a number of cases this one time opportunity to generate money credits will suffice to incentivise a wide range of innovations. Not only will producers profit sufficiently but so will buyers who may then enjoy a first-mover advantage over their competitors. The market model may thus limitedly apply to free software regarding the initial one-off distribution.

More often, however, the development of software is an incremental process that greatly benefits from inputs of various sources evading the capabilities and control of a single firm. Nor is the conventional market an adequate institution to deal with the small individual inputs although these no doubt amount to gains from trade. The costs of assessing the merit of each contribution and the institution of a due compensation system are often prohibitively high. We have also seen that it is impractical if not impossible to draw complete contracts over software to deal with these contingencies. Thus a much more prominent way of accounting for credits in free software is a different one. Surprisingly, it consists of no more than the mere mentioning of the names of contributors in the software itself as well as communications regarding the same. This is a sufficient means of attributing contributions to the persons that have made them (Fisk 2006). The subsequent judging of the merits of individual contributions is a dynamic process both within the project itself and the adoption of the software by third parties that may, again, be observed by non-involved parties. A contribution of high value will often find its way into a project subject to the scrutiny of other

---

11 Monitoring is costly and thus imperfect. However, so is the judgement of quality of goods and services in markets. Also, note that in firms there may be other kinds of payments, not, incidentally, named incentives.

peers while a poor contribution will simply not be adopted, very much like low-quality goods will not easily be sold in a market. The crucial point is that those judgements are often made with far greater reference to actual merit than social status in hierarchies or markets.

Credits in free software projects – entries in the credits-file,[12] on the project website, in mailing lists, forums, etc. – are credits in an economic sense, as they serve to account for individual achievements in those projects. Indeed, the informal accounting institutions in free software projects may be regarded to be their central social institution. Informal credits in free software are thus no different than money. They can be redeemed or extinguished just like the more conventional sorts of credit such as banknotes or bills of exchange.

We may now look at how these credits are being redeemed as well as the limitations to their redemption that will add to their due discount rate. Most often, the credits obtained by successfully contributing to a free software project translate into social status within the project and its wider community, or goodwill with prospective clients or employers.

Priddat (2006) has interpreted the credits obtained by efforts in free software projects as a means of attaining higher status in those projects and related exclusive networks. Such status may, in fact, not even be bought with money whilst the commercial value of such status is unquestionable, involving easier access to central information and increased influence on project decisions. We may really speak of credit redemption here, since the credits will have to be renewed at some point in order to maintain the social position once achieved.

Lerner and Tirole (2002) have argued that the credits obtained from free software efforts may serve as a means of signalling one's professional skills to prospective employers. Since it is costly for an employer to judge the skills of an applicant directly he may depend on a more easily observable proxy to this end. For Lerner and Tirole this is what the credits obtained in free software accomplish. Note, again, that those credits may not generally be obtained in exchange for money. And that they lose some of their exchange value over time.

---

12 Typically, every free software contains a file called *credits.txt* that lists all its contributors. Further information will often be available in a history file and a changelog file. Even the complete history of every single code change in a free software may often be available from a public version control system based on the software system Subversion or CVS.

We have thus identified two well-established instances where credits obtained from efforts put into free software may be redeemed for other goods. Both arguments may be combined to a third more general way of redeeming credits. Involvement in free software will not only signal skills to prospective employers or help achieve social status in the community, it may create a sympathetic standing with clients or buyers in general. We have noted above that application providers often contribute to underlying free software platforms.[13] This is not only due to specific needs regarding their own applications but also serves as a means of signalling to buyers their knowledge and commitment to lowering the costs of adjacent goods. Also, someone who has proven intimacy with a certain platform will more easily be trusted to perform well at creating applications for this platform or providing other services (Grand et al. 2004).

We also note a more abstract and theoretical point about the beneficial effects of informal credits and incomplete contracts in free software. Most of the information technology that surrounds us is social by its very nature. Thus it gives rise to interactions that will often generate value in ways that are impossible to anticipate duly. Formal contracts and money transactions will effectively foreclose the full potential for users of those technologies to create such value by interacting with one another as they see fit. Accordingly, the social costs of formal systems of commerce will often exceed those of informal ones. Further, the development of social technology is inevitably endogenous to the social processes they shape. The making of those technologies is, thus, itself a social process that will best be governed by informal means as they allow greater flexibility and appropriation of technologies in ways unforeseeable by any single mind.

Hence it is both the complexity and the social nature of technology that make informal credit accounting in the creation of software superior. Importantly, the informal credits generated in free software easily qualify as means of commerce in that they account for credits with society at large obtained through efforts put into free software.

Limits to the Viability of Informal Credits in Free Software

The viability of informal contract and credit systems in free software has its limits, though. Those are shaped, particularly, by the relative costs and benefits of more formal systems in two principal respects: the micro-incentives or lack

---

13 See footnote 6 and accompanying text.

thereof created by the nature of credits obtained from contributing to free software, and the 'macro'-fit of those credits with the more money-oriented commercial contexts of free software.

The scope of redemption of free software credits is clearly limited to the contexts set out above. Put differently, the scope of debits available to redeem the credits obtained from free software development does not scale indefinitely. In fact, the returns from free software development may diminish very quickly as soon as we go beyond the immediate core developer group and the initial contributions that have set the scene, so to speak (Dalle and David 2005). Plus, wherever the costs of drawing more complete contracts are relatively low and the participants to the transactions in question are easily identified, a more formal credit system can become a more sensible strategy for all parties involved. Hence even the relatively large credits available for early and prominent involvement may be dwarfed by those available through formal money-based transactions.

As for the suitability of free software credits in a macro sense, there are areas in the field of free software and in fields closely related to it where the informal system of contracts and credits performs poorly compared to more formal systems. This may, again, be due to the better performance of money-based formal approaches. Quite often fields such as marketing or training are simply incompatible with the informal credits notion in that potential parties to transactions in those fields have no use whatsoever for the informal credits available in free software projects. This is particularly true for the following areas:

- creating comprehensive documentation

- integrating and testing with different environments

- offering support, services, such as customisation, and training.

It is no coincidence that the most important commercial business models in free software are support, services, training, dual-licensing and the offering of proprietary extensions that do not fall under the restrictive licensing obligations of the free software they build on. All those models largely build on formal contracts with customers and money payments, as well as the more informal credits obtained by involvement in the underlying free software projects. Effectively, the revenues obtained from these models help fund some of the more neglected areas in free software, such as documentation and exhaustive testing. Also, companies pursuing those business models play a vital role in the production of free software as they can afford the substantial money payments involved in obtaining certification, financing marketing efforts and offering insurance and warranty to customers.

Consequently, we find both informal and formal structures of contract and credit in the wider context of free software depending on their respective viability and relative performance.

Conclusion

Informal contractual relationships involving credits consisting of little more than public notes about respective individual involvements play an important role in free software. The viability of this surprising institutional framework builds on three premises:

- The binding and enforceable prohibition of appropriation by way of a free software licence that governs the legal requirements of every receiver of the software.

- The prohibitive costs of complete contract and money credit institutions in the development of large complex software making viable an incomplete contract based system of informal credits despite the due discounts on such credits.

- The viability of business models partly based on complete contracts and money payments in the field of free software that allows support of those areas in free software in which informal systems perform poorly. This model is particularly relevant with regard to the coding efforts involved in the development of free software. While the licensing terms are a vital means of foreclosing a proprietary direction of a project once it is free software, it is the relative superiority of informal relationships among a dispersed community of individuals in the development and use of free software that makes the model so successful. Similarly, there are areas in free software development where proprietary models are far better and tend to beat efforts organised in an informal manner. Principally, this is the case where the work on and around free software interfaces with more traditional institutional business structures such as professional services, marketing and support.

The credit model put forward in this chapter provides us with a unified means of understanding and modelling a wide array of free software development efforts and the incentives behind them. It also illuminates the fact that there are differences and respective strengths of informal and more formal means of commerce in software development and dissemination. Finally, it reminds us that in order to alleviate the divergence between private and public ends that is so often found in the context of information goods we may not necessarily resort to means of blunt government intervention, but much rather trust in informal, bottom-up, yet surprisingly potent institutions.

References

Assay, N.M. (2005). Open Source and the Commodity Urge: Disruptive Models for a Disruptive Development Process. In C. DiBona, D. Cooper and M. Stone (eds), *Open Sources 2.0: The Continuing Evolution*. London: O'Reilly. http://www.open-bar.org/docs/matt_asay_open_source_chapter_11-2004.pdf. Last accessed October 19 2010.

Bärwolff, M. (2006). Tight Prior Open Source Equilibrium. *First Monday* 11(1).   http://www.firstmonday.org/issues/issue11_1/barwolff/index.html. Last accessed October 19 2010.

Bauer, A. and M. Pizka (2003). The Contribution of Free Software to Software Evolution. In *Proceedings of the 6th IEEE International Workshop on Principles of Software Evolution (IWPSE03)*, 170–83. Los Alamitos, CA: IEEE Computer Society. http://www4.in.tum.de/publ/papers/mp03f.pdf.

Bessen, J.E. (2005). Open Source Software: Free Provision of Complex Public Goods. Working paper, Research on Innovation. http://www.researchoninnovation.org/opensrc.pdf. Last accessed October 19 2010.

Boldrin, M. and D.K. Levine (2002). Perfectly Competitive Innovation. Staff Report 303. Federal Reserve Bank of Minneapolis. http://ideas.repec.org/p/cpr/ceprdp/3274.html. Last accessed October 19 2010.

Bolton, G. and A. Ockenfels (2000). A Theory of Equity, Reciprocity and Competition. *American Economic Review* 100(1), 166–93.

Bowles, S. (2004). *Microeconomics: Behavior, Institutions, and Evolution*. Princeton: Princeton University Press.

Brooks Jr., F.P. (1995). *The Mythical Man-month: Essays on Software Engineering Anniversary Edition*. Reading: Addison-Wesley. First published in 1975.

Coase, R.H. (1937). The Nature of the Firm. *Economica* 4, 386–405.

Coase, R.H. (1960). The Problem of Social Cost. *Journal of Law and Economics* 3, 1–44. http://www.sfu.ca/~allen/CoaseJLE1960.pdf Last accessed October 19 2010.

Dalle, J.-M. and P.A. David (2005). Allocation of Software Development Resources in Open Source Production Mode. In J. Feller, B. Fitzgerald, S.A. Hissam, and K.R. Lakhani (eds), *Perspectives on Free and Open Source Software*, pp. 297–328. Cambridge, MA: The MIT Press.

Demil, B. and X. Lecocq (2006). Neither Market nor Hierarchy or Network: The Emerging Bazaar Governance. *Organization Studies* 27(10), 1447–66.

Diekmann, A. (2004). The Power of Reciprocity. *Journal of Conflict Resolution* 48(4), 487–505.

Durkheim, E. (1893). *De la division du travail social*. Paris: Presses Universitaires de France.

Economides, N. and E. Katsamakas (2005). Linux vs. Windows: A Comparison of Application and Platform Innovation Incentives for Open Source and Proprietary Software Platforms. Working Paper #05-07, NET Institute. http://opensource.mit.edu/papers/economideskatsamakas.pdf. Last accessed on October 19 2010.

Ellickson, R.C. (1991). *Order without Law: How Neighbors Settle Disputes*. Cambridge, MA: Harvard University Press.

Falk, A. and U. Fischbacher (2000). A Theory of Reciprocity. Working Paper, Institute for Empirical Research in Economics, University of Zurich.

Fehr, E. and S. Gächter (2000). Fairness and Retaliation: The Economics of Reciprocity. *The Journal of Economic Perspectives* 14(3), 159–81.

Fisk, C. (2006). Credit Where it's Due: The Law and Norms of Attribution. *Georgetown Law Journal* 95(1), 49–118.

Fleissner, P. (2006). Die Heilung der Achillesferse. In B. Lutterbeck, M. Bärwolff, and R.A. Gehring (eds), *Open Source Jahrbuch 2006. Zwischen Softwareentwicklung und Gesellschaftsmodell*, pp. 409–26. Berlin: Lehmanns Media.

Gehring, R.A. (2005). The Institutionalization of Open Source. *Poiesis und Praxis* 4(1), 54–73.

Ghosh, R.A. et al. (2006). Economic Impact of Open Source Software on Innovation and the Competitiveness of the Information and Communication Technologies (ICT) Sector in the EU. Final report, Contract ENTR/04/112, UNU-MERIT. Prepared for European Communities, http://www.flossimpact. eu/. Last accessed October 19 2010.

Grand, S., G. von Krogh, D. Leonard and W. Swap (2004). Resource Allocation Beyond Firm Boundaries: A Multi-level Model for Open Source Innovation. *Long Range Planning* 37, 591–610.

Grossman, S.J. and O.D. Hart (1986). The Costs and Benefits of Ownership: A Theory of Vertical and Lateral Integration. *Journal of Political Economy* 94(4), 691–719.

Hart, O.D. and J. Moore (1988). Incomplete Contracts and Renegotiation. *Econometrica* 56(4), 755–85.

Hayek, F.A. (1945). The Use of Knowledge in Society. *American Economic Review* 35(4), 519–30.

Henry, J.F. (2004). The Social Origins of Money: The Case of Egypt. In L.R. Wray (ed.), *Credit and State Theories of Money: The Contributions of A. Mitchell Innes*, pp. 79–98. Cheltenham: Edward Elgar.

Hudson, M. (2004). The Archeology of Money: Debt versus Barter Theories of Money's Origin. In L.R. Wray (ed.), *Credit and State Theories of Money: The Contributions of A. Mitchell Innes*, pp. 99–127. Cheltenham: Edward Elgar.

Iacobucci, E.M. and G.G. Triantis (2007). Economic and Legal Boundaries of Firms. *Virginia Law Review* 93(3), 515–70.

IDC (2004). Worldwide Linux 2004–2008 Forecast: Moving from Niche to Mainstream. IDC Study IDC #32424, IDC Software Consulting. Summary available at http://www.tc2l.ca/fileadmin/tc2l/media/pdf/IDC_linux_market_overview.pdf. Last accessed October 19 2010.

Ingham, G. (2004). The Emergence of Capitalist Credit Money. In L.R. Wray (ed.), *Credit and State Theories of Money: The Contributions of A. Mitchell Innes*, pp. 173–222. Cheltenham: Edward Elgar.

Innes, A. (1914). The Credit Theory of Money. *Banking Law Journal* 31, 151–68.

Lerner, J. and J. Tirole (2002). Some Simple Economics of Open Source. *Journal of Industrial Economics* 50(2), 197–234.

Malinowski, B. (1922). *Argonauts of the Western Pacific: An Account of Native Enterprise and Adventure in the Archipelagoes of Melanesian New Guinea.* London: Routledge & Kegan Paul.

Osterloh, M., S. Rota, and B. Kuster (2002). Open Source Software Production: Climbing on the Shoulders of Giants. Working paper, The University of Zurich. http://opensource.mit.edu/papers/osterlohrotakuster.pdf. Last accessed October 19 2010.

Pigou, A.C. (1932). *The Economics of Welfare* (4th edn). London: Macmillan.

Priddat, B.P. (2006). Open Source als Produktion von Transformationsgütern. In B. Lutterbeck, M. Bärwolff and R. A. Gehring (eds), *Open Source Jahrbuch 2006. Zwischen Softwareentwicklung und Gesellschaftsmodell*, pp. 109–21. Berlin: Lehmanns Media. http://www.opensourcejahrbuch.de.

Rosenberg, S. (2007). *Dreaming in Code: Two Dozen Programmers, Three Years, 4,732 Bugs, and One Quest for Transcendent Software.* New York: Crown Publishers.

Shah, S. and M. Tripsas (2004). When do User-innovators Start Firms? Towards a Theory of User Entrepreneurship. University of Illinois Working Paper 04-0106, University of Illinois. http://userinnovation.mit.edu/papers/Shah-Tripsas%20_2_%20%204-9-04.pdf. Last accessed October 19 2010.

Shapiro, C. and H.R. Varian (1999). *Information Rules: A Strategic Guide to the Network Economy*. Cambridge, MA: Harvard Business School Press.

Smith, L.K. (2006). Synergies and Opportunities: Open Source and Commercial Vendors—A Study of the Relational Database Market. Master's thesis, Technische Universität Berlin. Published as book on demand at http://www.lulu.com/content/516973. Last accessed October 19 2010.

Stiglitz, J.E. (1999). Knowledge as a Global Public Good. In I. Kaul, I. Grunberg and M.A. Stern (eds), *Global Public Goods: International Cooperation in the 21st Century*, pp. 308–25. Oxford: Oxford University Press.

Tripsas, M. (2006). Customer Preference Discontinuities: A Trigger for Radical Technological Change. Harvard Business School Working Paper 02-028. Cambridge, MA: Harvard Business School. http://www.people.hbs.edu/mtripsas/articles/Tripsas%20final%20MDE%20April%202006.pdf Last accessed October 19 2010

Von Hippel, E. (2005). *Democratizing Innovation*. Cambridge, MA: MIT Press.

PART III

OSS Success, Measurement and Metrics

Introduction

As outlined in Part II of this book, as participation in OSS communities continues to grow, so does researchers' interest. While the issue of individual motivation for participation represents a frequent research interest, another research interest is what factors influence the success of OSSP and how we can measure success in this specific context.

Understanding the issue of information systems success and measurement is not new. It has occupied and continues to occupy the highest priority in the MIS research agenda. In Part III, *OSS Success, Measurement and Metrics*, three chapters provide an analysis of this challenging question in the specific context of OSSP.

The first chapter summarizes the results from three studies that have addressed the question of what factors influence the success of smaller OSSP across dimensions important to varied audiences. In the second chapter, using the Delone and McLean model of information systems success, one of the most commonly cited models in this area of research, the authors develop a set of measures to assess project effectiveness in the context of OSS and illustrate OSSP effectiveness through data collected on SourceForge.

Finally, Chapter 9 discusses the specific case of very small OSS projects, investigating how we can define success in their case and comparing how they are different from other projects.

7

Studies of Success in Open Source Software Projects[1]

Katherine Stewart

Introduction

Open source software (OSS) development is a phenomenon that has experienced a great deal of growth over the past decade, garnering attention among software developers; individual, organizational and governmental software users; and academic researchers in many disciplines. Much early and ongoing research attention has focused on understanding the performance of relatively mature projects such as Linux and Apache (Godfrey and Tu, 2000; Mockus et al., 2002). Understanding of issues affecting project performance in smaller and less mature OSS projects has received less attention and may be important for understanding how they evolve into larger projects or sustain themselves over time. This chapter summarizes a set of studies that have addressed the question of what factors influence the success of smaller OSS projects across dimensions important to varied audiences.

The overarching framework guiding the research program is depicted in Figure 7.1. The model includes two broad types of OSS success, *development success*, and *usage success*. Development success consists of success in attracting input to the project and success in producing project output. The former might be indicated, for example, by the number of people who work on the project or how many contributions they make, while the latter might be indicated by the amount of code released or an assessment of the code quality. Usage

---

1   Acknowledgments: The research described in this chapter was supported by the National Science Foundation award IIS-0347376. Any opinions, findings, and conclusions or recommendations expressed in this material are those of the author and do not necessarily represent the views of the National Science Foundation.

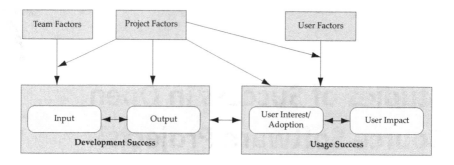

Figure 7.1   Research framework

success is composed of user interest/adoption, which might be indicated by a user gathering information about the software or downloading project files, and also user impact, which might be indicated by performance changes that result from use of the software.

Research suggests many potential factors that may influence both development and usage success. For the purpose of this chapter these factors are grouped into three categories: those associated with the development team (Team Factors), those associated with the product of the team (Project Factors), and those associated with users of the product (User Factors). Propositions regarding the relationships depicted in Figure 7.1 are discussed in Stewart (2004).

The remainder of this chapter summarizes findings of three studies, each designed to explore a part of the framework proposed in Figure 7.1. The first study focuses mainly on the influence of three kinds of team factors on development success measures. The team factors of interest are adherence to OSS ideology, communication quality within a team, and trust within a team. The second study explores how a project factor, development status, moderates the relationships among the team factors in Study 1 and different measures of development success. The third study focuses mainly on the role that project factors, license restrictiveness and project sponsorship, have on both development success and usage success. The chapter concludes by discussing research in progress to build on the finding in these three studies and to explore the impact of user factors.

Study 1: The Role of Ideology in Development Success

This first study was motivated by questions raised about how OSS development teams function successfully in the absence of formal controls (cf. Gallivan, 2001). Anecdotal evidence pointed to the importance of the OSS ideology in facilitating OSS teams' success, and the importance of ideology in general is supported by research in other settings that has shown the impacts that ideology may have on individuals, teams, and organizations (Barker, 1993; Kirsch, 1997). In Stewart and Gosain (2006c) we developed a framework of the OSS community ideology and investigated how ideological components influenced OSS team development success in 67 projects sampled from SourceForge. Figure 7.2 depicts the relationships studied in this research. This figure is based on Figure 7.1 in Stewart and Gosain (2006c), but modified to show how the research fits within the framework displayed in Figure 7.1.

Fifteen individual ideological components were identified from prior work and qualitative data sources, and OSS project administrators were surveyed about their teams' adherence to each ideological component. Data were also gathered on perceptual and objective measures of development success, including team size and effort and task completion. Factor analysis indicated that the 15 ideological components grouped into a smaller number of constructs representing different kinds of values, beliefs, and norms. *OSS collaborative values* revolve around the positive attitudes toward helping, sharing, and cooperation with others. *OSS individual values* focused on the benefit that individuals reap

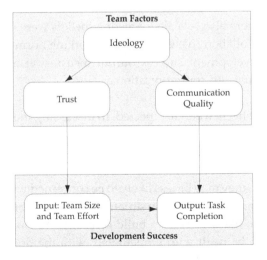

Figure 7.2   Study 1 research model

from OSS participation including learning, gaining technical knowledge, and building reputation. *OSS process beliefs* concerned the appropriate process to be used for fixing bugs, maintaining code quality, and status attainment. *OSS freedom beliefs* were those regarding the importance of freedom to outcomes, including freedom of information and of software. The three norms included in the study (against forking, for providing named credit for contributions, and for following distribution procedures) were adopted independently by OSS teams rather than constituting a larger construct.

Drawing on the literatures on virtual teams and identification, the study argued that adherence to these ideological components would influence development success mainly due to effects on trust and communication quality within the teams. The main thesis was that the tenets of the OSS ideology motivate behaviors that enhance cognitive trust and communication quality and encourage identification with the project team, which enhances affective trust. Leveraging the literature on virtual teams, cognitive and affective trust and communication quality were then argued to affect development success.

RESULTS OF STUDY 1

With the exception of the distribution norm, each of the ideological components played a significant role in determining development success. For collaborative values, individual values, the forking norm, the named credit norm, and process beliefs, the overall pattern of results supported arguments that these ideological components are important to success because of the positive impacts they have on trust and communication quality within the teams. However, two sets of negative effects were also revealed. Freedom beliefs were shown to have only negative effects. Collaborative values and the forking norm had direct negative effects on the development success output measure in addition to positive effects through trust and communication quality.

The negative effects were unexpected. In discussing these effects, the study speculated that negative effects of collaborative values and the forking norm could be a result of these ideological components imposing a "consensus-building cost." If team members believe that forking is acceptable (i.e. they go against the norm), they may be less likely to be concerned with avoiding conflict or building consensus. As a result, in situations involving conflicting ideas, these teams may be less likely to wait to build consensus before completing a task. Instead, tasks can be dealt with immediately with the option for disagreeing members to potentially fork the project.

Similarly, the more a team subscribes to collaborative values, the more they focus on attending to the needs of team members, which may detract from a focus on the task. Rather than closing task requests quickly, the team may spend time trying to build consensus on how tasks should be handled. The overall interpretation is that there may be a trade-off involved in fostering these ideological components: the positive affective trust built by these components helps to make the group membership valuable to developers and encourage their input, however output is slowed because of the increased desire to build consensus.

Higher levels of adherence to the freedom beliefs negatively impacted communication quality, cognitive trust, and team effort. The study suggests that one explanation for this pattern of effects may be that the strength of such beliefs could drive individuals to participate more broadly by spreading their effort across multiple projects, reducing their contribution to any one. That is, those who believe strongly in freedom as a crucial aspect of software development may be driven more by a desire to act as agents of social change than they are by the desire to further the objectives of a particular project. This could lead to reduced effort for the project. Because members' attention is spread across many projects the timing of their participation in any one may also be less predictable thereby reducing cognitive trust and communication quality. An alternative explanation could be that those who subscribe to the freedom beliefs also believe that users should take greater responsibility for fixing or changing the code as needed, and thus they are less inclined to address tasks requested by others. Developing and testing explanations for these unexpected effects may be one fruitful avenue for continued research on the role that ideology plays in determining OSS development success.

Study 2: The Moderating Role of Development Stage in Success

Building on Study 1, we leveraged data from the same set of projects to investigate how the relationships between team climate variables (ideology and trust) and success outcomes varies with the development stage of a project. Results of this study are reported fully in Stewart and Gosain (2006d). Figure 7.3 is a modified version of Figure 7.1 in that article, showing how the research fits within the framework shown previously in Figure 7.1. Dotted lines are used to differentiate moderating from direct effects.

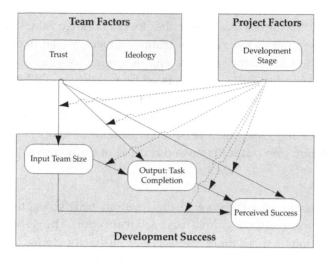

Figure 7.3   Study 2, moderating effect of development stage

OSS projects are typically categorized as being in stages: planning, pre-alpha development, alpha testing, beta testing, production, and mature. Stages prior to the beta testing stage are those during which developers are most focused on designing, building, and basic testing of the intended functionality; during the beta stage the focus is on user trial and testing to uncover and remove bugs; and in later stages the tested software is considered to be stable. The main thesis developed and tested in this study is that the development stage plays an important moderating role in determining both actual development success outcomes and subjective perceptions of such outcomes.

MODERATING EFFECTS ON THE RELATIONSHIPS AMONG TYPES OF SUCCESS

Perceived success is included in the model because research studies often rely on perceptions of performance as a proxy for actual performance, thus knowing if such perceptions reflect different kinds of actual performance at different times may be important. Development input and output success measures may provide project administrators with objective information to "calibrate" (Alba and Hutchinson, 2000) their subjective assessment of success. Work on calibration in psychology has developed models suggesting that people internalize the associations between cues and events in the world (Bjorkman, 1994; Gigerenzer et al., 1991), and draw upon this internalized knowledge when making judgments (Brenner, 2003). Objective indicators of performance such as task completion (output) and developer team size (input) constitute external cues that may enable project administrators to evaluate their success. The study argues that the availability and perceived relevance of these objective indicators varies across project stages such that input measures of success have a stronger effect on subjective assessments in early stages and output measures have a stronger effect in later stages.

The relationship between the actual success measures is also argued to be affected by development stage. One reason to expect a moderating effect is found in the software engineering literature that suggests client management and project management capabilities accumulate over time, resulting in improved project performance (Whang, 1995). Ethiraj et al. (2005) draw upon the dynamic capabilities perspective to suggest that capabilities tend to evolve over time to reflect the joint effects of passive learning-by-doing and deliberate investments in learning and making improvements. Based on this line of work the study argues that the relationship between development success on the input side and development success in terms of output should be stronger in later development stages than in earlier stages. In other words, at later stages the team will be more effective in converting input to output.

MODERATING EFFECTS ON THE RELATIONSHIPS BETWEEN TEAM FACTORS AND SUCCESS

In the early stages of a project, formalized procedures and work routines, clear project goals, and a track record of success may all be lacking. Weaknesses in these areas may inhibit development work because the lack of control makes coordination difficult. Trust and shared ideology may substitute as mechanisms to facilitate progress (Bergquist and Ljungberg, 2001; Kirsch et al., 2002). Thus the paper argues that the influence of team climate variables such as trust and ideology on development output will be stronger in earlier development stages.

In addition to having a greater effect on development output in early stages, the study argues that positive team climate may be expected to have a stronger effect on input by helping to attract and retain developers in early stages. Developers may associate and remain with a project for many reasons including the utility of the software produced, learning and reputational benefits that may accrue from participation, and psychological benefits derived from membership (Hann et al., 2002; Hars and Ou, 2002). The latter may be most important in early stages before the project has established a high level of utility or the recognition sufficient to create reputation benefits. Thus attracting and retaining developers in early stages may rely more on having a positive team climate whereas in later stages having clear goals and a track record may also contribute to developer attraction and retention.

RESULTS OF STUDY 2

Results of partial least squares (PLS) analysis supported the overall thesis underlying the research model, which was that the dynamics of success in OSS projects change as projects move through different stages. However, results of specific hypothesis tests were mixed, supporting some of the hypothesized relationships but also revealing some unexpected findings.

Consistent with expectations, the output measure of development success had the most positive effect on perceived success in later development stages and the input measure had the most positive effect in earlier stages. These effects support the argument that administrators calibrate their assessments to objective measures but that the relevance of input and outcome measures to that calibration changes over time. The input measure also had a more positive effect on the output measure in later stages than in early stages, however the overall effect was negative. While the study did not hypothesize the direction of a main effect, intuitively one might expect greater input to lead to greater output. The fact that it did not may be because in OSS projects a larger number of developers implies the availability of more labor to work on tasks, but it also means more tasks will be generated because more people are scrutinizing the project. The findings are interpreted as implying that in early stages the efforts of developers in identifying new tasks outstrips their efforts in completing those tasks but in later stages task identification and completion even out.

The study hypothesized that team climate variables would have more positive effects on both input and output success measures in early as opposed to later development stages because the importance of climate variables would be reduced as other process variables such as work routines became more established. The study discusses reverse causality as a possible explanation for mixed results of these hypothesis tests. For example, contrary to expectations, the results indicated that shared ideology had a negative overall relationship to both input and output success variables, and it was more negative in early as opposed to later stages. The negative main effect on input might be explained because, all else being equal, larger groups will naturally have greater diversity among members in terms of beliefs, values, and norms. However over time as the team works together and the project moves to later development stages members may develop higher levels of shared ideology. For output, the results could imply that groups with stronger shared ideology invest more time in attending to the social needs of the members at the expense of task completion. The study points out that future research is needed to better understand these effects as the data collected in this work could not differentiate among competing alternative explanations.

Finally, the model proposed that the effect of team climate variables on perceived success would be reduced in later stages as objective information to calibrate judgments accumulated and attribution biases were reduced. Results indicated that shared ideology did follow this pattern; however, there was a marginally significant interaction effect in the opposite direction for affective trust, showing that the positive effect of affective trust on perceived success was stronger in later stages. The mixed results here indicate that aspects of team climate may vary in their impact over time and future research should utilize more granular measures to better establish the role—or lack thereof—of team climate in biasing subjective judgments of success.

Study 3: Roles of Licensing and Sponsorship in Success

In the third study (Stewart et al., 2006a), we shifted from a focus on team factors and development success to explore the role of project factors impacting both development and usage success. The portion of the overall framework explored in this study is depicted in Figure 7.4, which is based on Figure 7.1 in Stewart et al. (2006a).

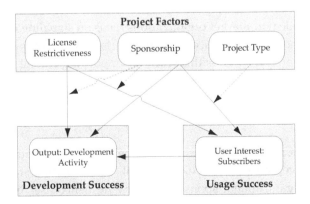

Figure 7.4   Study 3 research model

This study focused on exploring the effects of license restrictiveness and organizational sponsorship on two success measures: project development activity (an output measure captured by counting new software releases in a fixed period) and the interest in the project among users and potential users (measured as a number of people who subscribed to announcements about the project). The study developed the argument that for a project to be successful on the development output dimension, characteristics of the project must be aligned with developer motivations (because output depends on developer input, as shown in the prior studies). Similarly, the article argued that in order to be successful in garnering user interest, characteristics of OSS projects must signal to potential users that the project is likely to provide a high level of overall utility.

Prior work suggested the importance of restrictiveness of the project's OSS license (Lerner and Tirole, 2002a). In particular, two restrictions are highlighted: the requirement that modified versions of the software also be open (often referred to as a "copyleft" provision) and the requirement that the code be combined only with other programs distributed under licenses that share the first requirement (often referred to as a "viral" provision). This study distinguishes between licenses that have both of these provisions (*restrictive*) and those that have neither or only one of the provisions (*non-restrictive*).

The second project factor, organizational sponsorship, captures the fact that some but not all OSS projects are affiliated with a formal organization such as a company or a university. Institutional theory suggests an important distinction between organizations that tend to be market driven, such as for-profit firms, and those that are less so, such as government and educational organizations (cf. Scott, 1998). Market organizations are driven by economic needs and incentives and thus focus on signaling product characteristics that consumers are willing to pay for, while non-market organizations focus on signaling conformity with institutional norms or practices to enhance legitimacy (Downs, 1967; Scott, 1998; Thompson, 1967). Thus this study distinguished among three categories of sponsorship: no sponsor, market sponsor, and non-market sponsor.

INFLUENCES ON USER INTEREST

The study leveraged work on consumer behavior (e.g., Zeithaml, 1988) and technology acceptance (e.g., Venkatesh et al., 2003) to understand how license choice and organizational sponsorship may influence user interest. The use of restrictive licenses may affect users' perception of the costs and benefits of using software in at least two ways. First, while requirements to open modified versions and combine software only with similarly licensed software act to maintain the "openness" of the code, they are restrictive in the sense that they limit what a user can do with the software. These restrictions may constrain commercialization of OSS applications (Lerner and Tirole, 2002a; West, 2003). In doing so, they may significantly reduce the perceived usefulness of the software among potential users seeking to advance commercial interests. Second, perceived usefulness may be reduced by restrictive licenses in that such licenses limit potential users' ability to employ the code in conjunction with software distributed under a less restrictive license. An important feature of software is its compatibility with other applications. The restrictions imposed by a license's viral provision may inhibit the exploitation of some cross-application compatibility, consequently reducing potential gains that could otherwise be realized.

Organizational sponsorship may also effect users' perceptions of the likely utility of software in at least two ways. First, there may be a direct effect on software quality because sponsors could devote resources to the project. Second, organizational sponsorship may be a salient extrinsic cue for evaluating OSS. Perceived costs associated with using software include price (which for most OSS is close to zero), and also such factors as maintenance time and effort expended in using the software in the future. Organizational sponsorship may imply the availability of technical support, upgrades, and other resources that may be needed over the long term. A greater degree of uncertainty may exist regarding the availability of resources or services for non-sponsored OSS projects.

Considering the type of sponsor for a project, market organizations may be more driven to find ways to capitalize on an OSS project, while non-market organizations may be more motivated to conform to the norms associated with OSS development. The study hypothesized that potential users in the open source community may therefore be more likely to use an OSS sponsored by a non-market organization than one sponsored by a market organization because the former will be seen as less likely to attempt to derive rents from users and more likely to act in ways congruent with the OSS ideology. Sponsorship by a market organization may introduce in the minds of potential users the threat that the OSS could in the future be "hijacked" by commercial interests (Lerner and Tirole, 2002a). When the sponsoring entity is an organization whose purpose is seen as enhancing social welfare (e.g., a government organization), such concerns may be lessened.

INFLUENCES ON DEVELOPMENT OUTPUT

The study leveraged the work on motivation in OSS development to hypothesize effects of licensing and sponsorship on development success. Prior work suggested that OSS contributors find programming intrinsically motivating, deriving feelings of competence and self-determination from the activity itself or from helping others (Crowston and Scozzi, 2002; Hars and Ou, 2002); that they contribute to satisfy their personal needs for software (Hars and Ou, 2002; Raymond, 2001; Von Hipple, 2001); and that programmers contribute to enhance their skills and reputations (Krishnamurthy, 2002); possibly with the expectation of future returns (DiBona et al., 1999; Hann et al., 2002; Hars and Ou, 2002; Lerner and Tirole, 2002b).

Licensing may be important to maintain motivations related to reputation and career concerns and producing something of personal use. Lerner and Tirole (2002c) suggested that restrictive licenses serve to protect the interests of developers by limiting the possibility of commercial exploitation of their contributions by third parties. Commercialization of an open source project may be undesirable from the contributors' viewpoint because it may reduce the market for the open version of the project, thereby reducing visibility of contributions and possible reputation benefits.

Sponsorship could have both benefits and drawbacks in terms of project development activity. As noted above, a sponsor may provide resources such as paid workers thereby possibly enhancing development success. Yet an association with a market organization could dampen enthusiasm among volunteer developers because certain tenets of the open source culture seem to value independence from organizational constraints and, in some cases, disdain of profit motives (Stewart and Gosain, 2006d). Non-market sponsors are more likely to be seen as having goals consistent with the ideology of OSS developers and may therefore avoid this problem. Thus, non-market organizations may provide resources to a project without being seen by potential volunteer developers as presenting a threat of commercialization, and the study hypothesized a positive effect of non-market sponsorship on development success.

RESULTS OF STUDY 3

The study hypotheses were tested using longitudinal data on 138 OSS projects. As expected, there were overall positive effects on user interest for using non-restrictive licenses and for sponsorship. However, results indicated that these effects were mainly driven by the large difference between non-market sponsored projects that used restrictive versus non-restrictive licenses, with a marginal, smaller effect between the two license types for non-sponsored projects. License restrictiveness had no effect for market-sponsored projects and market-sponsored projects did not attract significantly more user interest than non-sponsored projects.

An interpretation of the pattern of results suggested in the study is that sponsorship trumps licensing in terms of its impact on users' perceptions regarding the likelihood of the software remaining free of commercial control; the benefits and drawbacks that users infer from market sponsorship essentially cancel each other out. In other words, the benefit that market sponsorship may bring based on the perceived availability of future support may be cancelled out by the concurrent expectation that costs may be higher as the sponsor seeks to generate rents from the project. Similarly, the potential benefits of non-restrictive licensing in market-sponsored projects may be cancelled by the expectation that the sponsor will control the future direction of the project for its own benefit.

Sponsorship was also of varying importance to user interest across project types. Results were mostly consistent with the reasoning that the user concerns addressed by sponsorship (e.g., support) are more relevant for software that generally has more diverse uses (e.g., utilities) than for software that generally has narrower uses (e.g., software development projects).

DRIVERS OF DEVELOPMENT ACTIVITY

A main effect of initial user interest on the output measure lent support to the argument that having an audience enhances developers' motivation to work on a project and thereby increases development success. An interaction effect of licensing and sponsorship on output indicated that while the differences were in the expected direction, the effects of restrictive licensing on development success for non-sponsored projects and for market-sponsored projects was insignificant. The effect was significant and in the opposite direction for non-market-sponsored projects.

While this pattern is consistent with the interaction hypothesis, we had not expected the effect of licensing for non-market organizations to reverse (only to decrease). In the study, this result is interpreted as follows. For non-sponsored projects the situation is relatively simple: there are no organizational motives to consider, and all developers are volunteers without organization-instilled motives, therefore the logic leading to the hypothesis that restrictive licensing elicits greater development activity holds. When a market sponsor is present and using a restrictive license, cues as to the project's future are somewhat at odds in that the license indicates the software will remain open whereas the sponsor's motives may bring that intention into question. Thus the difference between license types may be reduced. The presence of a non-market sponsor may alleviate concerns as to the project's future in the same way that a restrictive license would, such that the restrictive license is not perceived as necessary to protect the developers' interests. Thus they are, because of their additional role as users, attracted to the greater flexibility associated with non-restrictive licenses. These explanations warrant development and testing in future work.

Conclusions and Ongoing Research

Taken together, results of the three studies indicate significant support for the propositions implied in the overarching framework in Figure 7.1, while also pointing to many areas that remain to be explored. One conclusion supported by the results of the three studies is that attracting development input to a project is a key to enhancing other kinds of success. If the OSS phenomenon continues to grow, more development input will be needed to sustain many OSS projects. In this case, engaging previously under-utilized populations of developers may become a route to success. One such population consists of female software developers. Surveys and anecdotal evidence have indicated that women have had very low levels of participation in OSS (Ghosh et al., 2002). In response to this fact, several large projects have created "women's groups" to try to enhance women's participation, and we have begun a research effort to study the roles played by these groups (Stewart et al., 2007).

The important role of development output success has also been highlighted in the three studies, and one may conclude that objective indicators of output success are influential to both developer and users perceptions about, and behaviors toward, projects. Given the importance of development output, we are engaged in ongoing research to understand how other important output indicators such as the structure of OSS code evolve over time (Stewart et al., 2006b).

The least explored aspect of the model in Figure 7.1 is the role of users and the determinants of usage success. While Study 3 began to address these areas, our current work is expanding on this by investigating the role that users play in building the absorptive capacity of a project team (Daniel et al., 2006). Early results indicate the importance of users in acquiring relevant knowledge and transferring knowledge to the development team.

Overall, the work described in this chapter has aimed to build understanding of how and why relatively small OSS projects succeed (or fail). This research program complements and extends the work of many others exploring similar questions (e.g., Bonaccorsi and Rossi, 2003; Crowston et al., 2003; Hars and Ou, 2002; Zhao and Elbaum, 2003). Building an understanding of the critical success factors in OSS is important both because the OSS phenomenon has become a large economic and social force, and because understanding success in this context may help us to make recommendations for other closely related work contexts such as proprietary software development work or open content creation (e.g., Wikipedia). Much research remains to be done, and we hope that these studies may serve as a stepping stone for others.

References

Alba, J. and Hutchinson, W. (2000). Knowledge Calibration: What Consumers Know and What They Think They Know. *Journal of Consumer Research*, 27: 324–44.

Barker, J.R. (1993). Tightening the Iron Cage – Concertive Control in Self-Managing Teams. *Administrative Science Quarterly*, 38(3): 408–37.

Bergquist, M. and Ljungberg, J. (2001). The Power of Gifts: Organizing Social Relationships in Open Source Communities. *Information Systems Journal*, 11(4): 305–20.

Bjorkman, M. (1994). Internal Cue Theory: Calibration and Resolution of Confidence in General Knowledge. *Organizational Behavior and Human Decision Processes*, 57: 386–405.

Bonaccorsi, A. and Rossi, C. (2003). Why Open Source Software Can Succeed. *Research Policy*, 32(7): 1243.

Brenner, L. (2003). A Random Support Model of the Calibration of Subjective Probabilities. *Organizational Behavior and Human Decision Processes*, 90: 87–110.

Crowston, K. and Scozzi, B. (2002). Open Source Software Projects as Virtual Organizations: Competency Rallying for Software Development. *IEE Proceedings Software*, 149(1): 3–17.

Crowston, K., Annabi, H. and Howison, J. (2003). Defining Open Source Software Project Success. Paper presented at the International Conference on Information Systems, December, Seattle, WA.

Daniel, S., Agarwal, R. and Stewart, K.J. (2006). An Absorptive Capacity Perspective on Open Source Software Development Group Performance. Paper presented at the 27th International Conference on Information Systems, December, Milwaukee, WI.

DiBona, C., Ockman, S. and Stone, M. (1999). *Open Sources: Voices from the Open Source Revolution*. Sebastopol, CA: O'Reilly.

Downs, A. 1967. *Inside Bureaucracy*. Boston, MA: Little, Brown.

Ethiraj, S.K., Kale, P., Krishnan, M.S. and Singh, J.V. (2005). Where Do Capabilities Come from and How Do They Matter? A Study in the Software Services Industry. *Strategic Management Journal*, 26(1): 25–45.

Gallivan, M.J. (2001). Striking a Balance between Trust and Control in a Virtual Organization: A Content Analysis of Open Source Software Case Studies. *Information Systems Journal*, 11(4): 277–304.

Ghosh, R.A., Glott, R., Krieger, B. and Robles, G. (2002). Free/Libre Open Source Software: Survey and Study, Workshop on Advancing the Research Agenda on Free/Open Source Software. Maastricht: International Institute of Infonomics, University of Maastricht, Netherlands.

Gigerenzer, G., Hoffrage, U. and Kleinbolting, H. (1991). Probabalistic Mental Models: A Brunswikian Theory of Confidence. *Psychological Review*, 98: 506–28.

Godfrey, M.W. and Tu, Q. (2000). Evolution in Open Source Software: A Case Study. Paper presented at the International Conference on Software Maintenance, October, San Jose, California.

Hann, I.-H., Roberts, J., Slaughter, S.A. and Fielding, R. (2002). Economic Incentives for Participating in Open Source Software Projects. Paper presented at the 23rd International Conference on Information Systems, December, Barcelona, Spain.

Hars, A. and Ou, S. (2002). Working for Free? Motivations for Participating in Open Source Projects. *International Journal of Electronic Commerce*, 6(3): 25–39.

Kirsch, L.J. (1997). Portfolios of Control Modes and is Project Management. *Information Systems Research*, 8(3): 215–39.

Kirsch, L.J., Sambamurthy, V., Ko, D.-G. and Purvis, R.L. (2002). Controlling Information Systems Development Projects: The View from the Client. *Management Science*, 48(4): 484–98.

Krishnamurthy, S. (2002). Cave or Community? An Empirical Examination of 100 Mature Open Source Projects. *First Monday*, 7(6). http://131.193.153.231/www/issues/issue7_6/krishnamurthy/index.html, Last accessed on October 19 2010.

Lerner, J. and Tirole, J. (2002a). The Scope of Open Source Licensing, working papers, http://idei.fr/doc/wp/2003/scope_open_source.pdf . Last accessed on October 19 2010.

Lerner, J. and Tirole, J. (2002b). Some Simple Economics of Open Source. *Journal of Industrial Economics*, 50(2): 197–234.

Lerner, J. and Tirole, J. (2002c). The Scope of Open Source Licensing, working paper.

Mockus, A., Fielding, R.T. and Herbsleb, J.D. (2002). Two Case Studies of Open Source Software Development: Apache and Mozilla. *ACM Transactions on Software Engineering and Methodology*, 11(3): 309–46.

Prahalad, C.K. and Krishnan, M.S. (1999). The New Meaning of Quality in the Information Age. *Harvard Business Review*, 77(5): 109–18.

Raymond, E.S. (2001). *The Cathedral and the Bazaar: Musing on Linux and Open Source by an Accidental Revolutionary*. Sebastopol, CA: O'Reilly.

Scott, W.R. (1998). *Organizations: Rational, Natural, and Open Systems* (4th edn). Upper Saddle River, NJ: Prentice-Hall.

Stewart, K.J. (2004). OSS Project Success: From Internal Dynamics to External Impact. Paper presented at the 4th Workshop on Open Source Software Engineering, May, Edinburgh, Scotland.

Stewart, K.J., Ammeter, A.P. and Maruping, L. (2006a). Impacts of License Choice and Organizational Sponsorship on User Interest and Development Activity in Open Source Software Projects. *Information Systems Research*, 17(2): 126–44.

Stewart, K.J., Darcy, D.P. and Daniel, S. (2006b). Opportunities and Challenges Applying Functional Data Analysis to the Study of Open Source Software. *Statistical Science*, 21(2): 167–78.

Stewart, K.J. and Gosain, S. (2006c). The Impact of Ideology on Effectiveness in Open Source Software Development Teams. *MIS Quarterly*, 30(2): 291–314.

Stewart, K.J. and Gosain, S. (2006d). The Moderating Role of Development Stage in Affecting Free/Open Source Software Project Performance. *Software Process Improvement and Practice*, 11(2): 177–91.

Stewart, K.J., Qiu, Y. and Bartol, K. (2007). Women's Groups in Open Source Software: Four Exploratory Case Studies, presented at the Academy of Management, August, Philadelphia, PA.

Thompson, J.D. (1967). *Organizations in Action*. New York: McGraw-Hill.

Venkatesh, V., Morris, M.G., Davis, G.B. and Davis, F. (2003). User Acceptance of Information Technology: Toward a Unified View. *MIS Quarterly*, 27(3): 425–78.

Von Hipple, E. (2001). Learning from Open Source Software. *Sloan Management Review*, Summer: 82–6.

West, J. (2003). How Open Is Open Enough? Melding Proprietary and Open Source Platform Strategies. *Research Policy*, 32(7): 1259–85.

Whang, S. (1995). Market Provision of Custom Software: Learning Effects and Low Balling. *Management Science*, 41(8): 1343–52.

Zeithaml, V.A. (1988). Consumer Perceptions of Price, Quality, and Value: A Means-End Model and Synthesis of Evidence. *Journal of Marketing*, 52: 2–22.

Zhao, L. and Elbaum, S. (2003). Quality Assurance under the Open Source Development Model. *Journal of Systems and Software*, 66: 65–75.

8

FLOSS Project Effectiveness Measures[1]

Kevin Crowston and James Howison

Introduction

In this chapter, we develop and illustrate measures of the effectiveness of FLOSS projects. FLOSS is a broad term used to embrace software that is developed and released under either a "free software" or an "open source" license. While the free software and the open source movements are distinct, both kinds of licenses allow users to obtain and distribute the software's original source without charge (software is "free as in beer") and to inspect, modify, and redistribute modifications to the source code. While the open source movement views these freedoms pragmatically (as a development methodology), the free software movement emphasizes the meaning of "free as in speech," which is captured by the French/Spanish *libre*, and one of their methods of supporting those freedoms is "copyleft," famously embodied in the General Public License, meaning that derivative works must be made available under the same license terms as the original. This chapter focuses on development practices in distributed work, which are largely shared across the movements. For example, many (though by no means all) FLOSS developers contribute to projects as volunteers without working for a common organization or being paid. We therefore use the acronym FLOSS to refer collectively to free/libre and open source software.

1   This research was partially supported by NSF Grants 03-41475, 04-14468 and 05-27457. Previous versions of this chapter have appeared as Crowston, K., Annabi, H. and Howison, J. (2003). Defining Open Source Software Project Success. In *Proceedings of the 24th International Conference on Information Systems (ICIS 2003)*, December, Seattle, WA; and Crowston, K., Howison, J. and Annabi, H. (2006). Information Systems Success in Free and Open Source Software Development: Theory and Measures. *Software Process—Improvement and Practice*, 11(2): 123–48.

It is important to develop measures of effectiveness for FLOSS projects for at least two reasons. First, having such measures should be useful for FLOSS project managers in assessing their projects. In some cases, FLOSS projects are sponsored by third parties, so measures are useful for sponsors to understand the return on their investment. Second, FLOSS is an increasingly visible and copied mode of systems development. Millions of users depend on FLOSS systems such as Linux and on the Internet, which is itself heavily dependent on FLOSS tools, but as Scacchi (2002a, p. 1) notes, "little is known about how people in these communities coordinate software development across different settings, or about what software processes, work practices, and organizational contexts are necessary to their success." An EU/NSF workshop on priorities for FLOSS research identified the need both for learning from open source modes of organization and production that could perhaps be applied to other areas and for a concerted effort on open source in itself, for itself (Ghosh 2002). But to be able to learn from teams that are working well, we need to have a definition of working well.

In the following sections of the chapter, we will first discuss several measures of project effectiveness, and then the procedure we used to obtain data with which to operationalize these measures, followed by the details of the analysis approach. We then present the results of this analysis and discuss the implications of these results. We then illustrate how these measures can be used to compare projects as part of a research study. We conclude with some suggestions for future research.

Measuring Project Effectiveness

The most commonly cited model for information systems success is DeLone and McLean (1992, 2002, 2003), shown in Figure 8.1. This model suggests six interrelated measures of success: system quality, information quality, use, user satisfaction, individual impact and organizational impact. Seddon (1997) proposed a related model that includes system quality, information quality, perceived usefulness, user satisfaction, and IS use. DeLone and McLean state that their model was built by considering "a process model [that] has just three components: the creation of a system, the use of the system, and the consequences of this system use" (2002, p. 87). We note that the measures included in their model focus on the use and consequences of the system and do not consider development. The choice of measures seems to be influenced by the relative ease of access to the use environment compared to the development environment

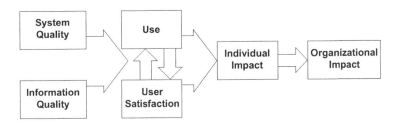

Figure 8.1   DeLone and McLean's model of information system success
Source: DeLone and McLean (1992, p. 87)

(especially true for packaged or commercial software). In the context of FLOSS though, researchers are frequently faced with the opposite situation, in that the development process is publicly visible and the use environment is difficult to study or even identify. We therefore start with a discussion of measures of success of the development process before considering the factors suggested by DeLone and McLean.

EFFECTIVENESS OF THE PROCESS OF SYSTEM DEVELOPMENT

For FLOSS projects, development is often considered an ongoing activity, as the project continues to release "often and early" (Raymond 1998). In other words, a FLOSS project is characterized by a continuing process of developers fixing bugs, adding features and releasing software. This characteristic of the FLOSS development process suggests a number of possible indicators of project effectiveness.

Number of Developers

First, since many FLOSS projects depend on volunteer developers, the ability of a project to attract and retain developers on an on-going basis is important for its success. Thus the *number of developers* involved in a project could be an indicator of success, both as an input for further develop and as an indirect measure of developer satisfaction with the project's processes and output. The number of developers can be measured in at least two ways. First, FLOSS development systems such as SourceForge (a free Web-based system that provides a range of tools to facilitate FLOSS development: http://sourceforge.net/) list *developers who are formally associated* with each project, meaning that they have been granted permission to add code (to be a "committer") to the source code control system (e.g., CVS). In projects hosted elsewhere, this measure could be performed by examination of CVS logs to see which developers commit code. In both cases though, this count would give an underestimate of developers for projects in which code is generally contributed on a mailing list and integrated by a few developers, suggesting the need for caution in developing this measure.

Second, examination of the mailing lists and other fora associated with projects can reveal the *number of individuals who actively participate* in development activities without being formally a developer on the project. This measure can help gauge the level of involvement of the users as indicated by involvement of the users in submitting bug reports and participating in the project mailing lists, which is important because most FLOSS projects are dependent on help from users to identify problems, post suggestions, and even provide support for other users.

Level of activity

More important than the sheer number of developers is their contribution to a project. Thus the *level of activity* of developers in submitting code and bug reports may be useful as an indicator of project success. For example, SourceForge computes and reports a measure of project activity based on the activities of developers. Researchers could also examine development logs for evidence of software being written and released.

Cycle time

Another measure related to the group activity is *time between releases*. In FLOSS development, there is a strong community norm to "release early and release often", which implies that an active release cycle is a sign of a healthy development process and project. For example, FreshMeat (a web-based system that tracks releases of FLOSS: http://freshmeat.net/) provides a "vitality score" (Stewart and Ammeter 2002) that assesses how recently a project has made an announcement of progress on the FreshMeat site (http://freshmeat.net/faq/view/27/). (However, there is some suggestion that these measures are being gamed by developers anxious to see their project highly rated, again suggesting the need for caution in interpreting the numbers.)

More detailed examination of bug-fixing and feature-request fulfillment activities can yield useful process data indicative of the project's status. Bug reports and feature requests are typically managed through a task-management system that records the developer and community discussion, permits labeling of priority items and sometimes includes informal "voting mechanisms" to allow the community to express its level of interest in a bug or new feature. The *time to close bugs* (or implement requested features) can be used as a measure of this aspect of project success.

PROJECT TEAM EFFECTIVENESS MEASURES

Finally, because the projects are ongoing, it seems important to consider the impact of a project on the abilities of the project team itself and its ability to continue or improve the development process. As Shenhar et al. (2001, p. 704) put it: "how does the current project help prepare the organization for future challenges?"

Employment opportunities

Some literature on the motivation of FLOSS developers suggests that developers participate to improve their employment opportunities (e.g., Lerner and Tirole 2000). Thus, one can consider *salary* (Hann et al. 2002) or *jobs acquired* through the involvement in a particular project as possible measures of success. For example, Hann et al. (2002) found that higher status within the Apache project was associated with significantly higher wages. Again, one might measure these indicators by surveying developers. While for a single developer, these measures are confounded with innate talent, training, luck, etc., aggregating across many developers and across time may provide a useful project-level measure of success.

Individual reputation

Similarly, literature also suggests that developers participating in FLOSS projects are rewarded with *reputation in the community*, and that this reputation is a sufficient reward for interaction. Kelty (2001) suggests that reputation might be measured through an analysis of credits located in source code (which he terms "greputation"). Alternative measures of FLOSS reputation might include the FLOSS communities' implementation of a "Web of Trust" at the community site Advogato (http://www.advogato.org/trust-metric. html) where developer status is conferred through peer review. Analyses of this kind of measure face the difficulty of tying the earning of reputation to the success of a particular project.

These measures might also be applied at the project level. Crowston, Howison and Annabi (2006) suggested *recognition* (e.g., mention on other sites) as a measure of project success. Similarly, another suggested measure was the *influence* of the product or project's process on other FLOSS groups and other commercial settings.

Knowledge creation

Projects can also lead to *creation of new knowledge* for individuals as well as on the group level (Arent and Nørbjerg 2000). Through their participation in a project, individual developers may acquire new procedural and programming skills that would benefit them on future projects. This effect could be measured by surveying the developers for their perceived learning.

In addition, following Grant's (1996) knowledge-based view of the firm, we view a firm (or in this case, a project) as a structure to integrate members' knowledge into products. In this view, the project's rules, procedures, norms, and existing products are a reflection of knowledge being created by the project activities. This *knowledge creation* can be measured by observing and qualitatively analyzing changes in the written rules and procedures over time and may be reflected and transferred through the development of systems for FLOSS project support, such as SourceForge and Savannah. Analysis of the development of interactions and support systems closely linked to a project might give some insight into this aspect of project success.

MEASURES OF THE OUTPUT OF SYSTEMS DEVELOPMENT

Two of the measures in the DeLone and McLean's model concern the product of the systems development process, namely systems quality and information quality. We first consider possible additional measures of this process step before turning to those measures.

Project completion

First, given the large number of abandoned projects (Ewusi-Mensah 1997), simply *completing a project* may be a sign of success. However, many FLOSS projects are continually in development, making it difficult to say when they are completed. Faced with this problem, Crowston and Scozzi (2002) instead measured success as the *progress of a project* from alpha to beta to stable status, as self-reported on SourceForge.

Second, another commonly used measure of success is whether the *project achieved its goals*. This assessment is typically made by a comparison of the project outcomes with the formal requirements specifications. However, FLOSS projects often do not have such specifications. Scacchi (2002b) examined the process of "requirements engineering" in open source projects and provided a comparison with the traditional processes (e.g., Jackson 1995; Davis 1990). He argues that rather than a formal process, FLOSS requirements are developed through what he terms "software informalisms", which do not result in agreed "requirements documentation" that could later be analyzed to see whether the project has met its goals. Scacchi's ethnography suggests that for FLOSS, goals will likely come from within through a discursive process centered on the developers. Therefore, a key measure for FLOSS may be simply *developer satisfaction* with the project, which could be measured by surveying developers. The developer community is much more clearly delineated than users, making such a survey feasible. Indeed, there have already been several FLOSS developer surveys (e.g., Ghosh 2002; Hertel et al. n.d.) though not on this topic specifically. Since in many projects there is a great disparity in the contribution of developers—a few developers contribute the bulk of the code (Mockus et al. 2000)—it may be desirable to weight developers' opinions in forming an overall assessment of a project.

System and information quality

Code quality has been studied extensively in software engineering. This literature provides many possible measures of the quality of software including understandability, completeness, conciseness, portability, consistency, maintainability, testability, usability, reliability, structuredness, and efficiency (Boehm et al. 1976; Gorton and Liu 2002). To this list might be added the *quality of the system documentation*. Code quality measures would seem to be particularly applicable for studies of FLOSS, since the code is publicly available. Indeed, a few studies have already examined this dimension. For example, Stamelos et al. (2002) suggested that FLOSS code is generally of good quality. Mishra, Prasad and Raghunathan (2002) offer an analytic model that suggests factors contributing to FLOSS code quality, such as number of developers, mix of talent level, etc. On the other hand, not many FLOSS systems include information per se, so the dimension of information quality seems to be less applicable.

MEASURES OF EFFECTIVENESS FROM THE USE OF A SYSTEM

User satisfaction

User satisfaction is an often-used measure of system success. For example, it is common to ask stakeholders if they felt a project was a success (e.g., Guinan et al. 1998). There is some data available regarding user satisfaction with FLOSS projects. For example, FreshMeat collects *user ratings* of projects. Unfortunately, these ratings are based on a non-random sample (i.e., users who take the time to volunteer a rating), making their representativeness suspect. Furthermore, we have observed that the scores seem to have low variance: in a recent sample of 59 projects, we found that scores ranged only from 7.47 to 9.07. It seems likely that users who do not like a piece of software simply do not bother to enter ratings. There do not seem to be any easily obtainable data on the related measures of perceived ease of use and usefulness (Davis 1989). *Opinions expressed on project mailing lists* are a potential source of qualitative data on these facets, though again there would be questions about the representativeness of the data.

In principle, it should be possible to *survey users* to collect their satisfaction with or perceptions of the software. However, to do so properly poses a serious methodological problem. Because most FLOSS projects are freely distributed through multiple channels, the population of users is unknown, making it impossible to create a true random sample of users. In this respect, FLOSS differs greatly from information systems developed in an organizational setting that have a clearly defined user population. The situation is also different than for the Web, another non-traditional systems environment, because with a Web site users are by definition the ones who visit the site, making the population effectively self-identifying. To achieve the same effect for FLOSS, the best solution might be to build the survey into the software, though doing so might annoy some users.

Use

Although there is some debate about its appropriateness (DeLone and McLean 2003; Seddon 1997), many studies employ system use as an indication of information systems success. For software for which use is voluntary, as is the case for most FLOSS, use seems like a potentially relevant indicator of the project's success. Unfortunately, actual usage data are available for only a few FLOSS projects. For example, Netcraft conducts a survey of Web server deployment (http://news.netcraft.com/archives/webserver_survey.html), which estimates the market share of different Web servers. Other projects that require some kind of network connection could potentially be measured in the same way (e.g., instant messaging or peer-to-peer file sharing clients), but this approach does not seem to be widely applicable. Many programs do check regularly for updated versions, which would provide a good measure of actual use, but these numbers do not seem to be publicly available.

Popularity

Rather than measuring actual use, it may be sufficient to count the actual or potential *number of users* of the software, which we label "popularity" (Stewart and Ammeter 2002). A simple measure of popularity is the *number of downloads* made of a project. These numbers are readily available from various sites. Of course not all downloads result in use, so variance in the conversion ratio will make downloads an unreliable indicator of use. Furthermore, because FLOSS can be distributed through multiple outlets, online as well as offline (e.g., on CDs), the count from any single source is likely to be quite unreliable as a measure of total users. A particularly important channel is "distributions" such as RedHat, SuSE or Debian. Distributions provide purchasers with pre-selected bundles of software packaged for easy installation and are often sold on a CD-ROM to obviate the need to download everything. Indeed, the most popular software might be downloaded only rarely because it is already installed on most users' machines and stable enough to not require the download of regular updates. Therefore, an important measure of popularity to consider is the package's *inclusion in distributions*. Crowston et al. (2006) found that developers consider porting of a product to different systems (especially to Windows), and requests for such ports as a measure of the success of the product. This theme might be considered a special case of popularity.

Other sources of data reflecting on users are available. Freshmeat provides a *popularity* measure for packages it tracks, though a better name might be "interest", as it is one step further removed from actual use. The measure is calculated as the geometric mean of subscriptions and two counts of page viewings of project information. Similarly, SourceForge provides information on the number of *page views of the information pages* for projects it supports.

Finally, it may be informative to measure use from perspectives other than that of an end user. In particular, the openness of FLOSS means that other projects can build on top of it. Therefore, one measure of a project's success may be that many other projects use it. *Package dependency* information between projects can be obtained from the package descriptions available through the various distributions' package management systems. Analysis of source code could reveal the *reuse of code* from project to project (though identifying the origin could be difficult).

Individual or organizational impacts

The final measures in DeLone and McLean's (1992) model are individual and organizational impacts for the users. Though there is considerable interest in the economic implications of FLOSS, these measures are hard to define for regular information systems projects and doubly hard for FLOSS projects, because of the problems defining the intended user base and expected outcomes. Therefore, these measures are likely to be unusable for most studies of individual FLOSS projects.

SourceForge Data on Effectiveness

In this chapter, we illustrate the use of a portfolio of measures in two ways. Specifically, we analyze four possible success measures, namely number of developers, number of mailing list participants, and number of downloads and page views for SourceForge projects in general and for a smaller sample of projects in more detail. These measures were chosen from the list above because they included both inputs (number of developers and users) and outputs (number of downloads and project Web page views).

Each of the proposed measures has good face validity, in the sense that a project that attracts developers and that many users download should be described as a success, especially if it continues to do so over time. However, we are interested in assessing how these measures relate to one another: do they measure the same construct or are they measuring different aspects of a multidimensional success construct? And most importantly, what insight do they provide into the nature of the development processes in the different projects?

In this section, we illustrate these measures using data about a large sample of FLOSS projects at a single point in time. To create a sample of FLOSS projects, we selected from projects hosted by SourceForge. As of May 2007, SourceForge claimed nearly 150,000 FLOSS projects on a wide diversity of topics.

Table 8.1   Descriptive statistics for selected effectiveness measures for
               the full sample of projects

Variable	Mean	Median	Standard deviation
downloads	10,760	52	423,103
page views	75,908	628	3,564,219
developers	2.35	1	4.45
unique message authentication	1.59	1	5.36

$N = 65,070$

Data for the four measures adopted are tracked by SourceForge and available for research from the SourceForge Research Data Archive (http://www.nd.edu/~oss/) and from the FLOSSmole project (http://ossmole.sourceforge.net; Howison et al. 2006). We obtained downloads, page views, and number of unique users in messages from the April 2007 dump in the SourceForge Research Data Archive (table stats_project_all). The developer count in this table counts active developers (though the definition of active is not given), so we obtained the total listed developer count from the April 2007 spider run in FLOSSmole. Projects that could not be spidered by FLOSSmole were eliminated from the sample. NULL values in the database dumps were replaced with 0s. The full dataset included 65,070 projects.

Clearly not all of these projects were suitable for our study: many are inactive and previous studies have suggested that many are in fact individual projects (Krishnamurthy 2002), as is borne out by the median of one developer. The low median number of downloads suggests that many of these projects are not actively distributing code. Since we are primarily interested in development practices in distributed groups, we restricted our analysis to projects that listed more than seven developers and had any downloads as of the date of the study. Being listed as a developer grants write access to the project's code base, so projects with multiple developers are ones that might be expected to experience significant coordination issues. Having downloads is indicative of a minimal level of development effort and having released files. Only 2,168 projects in our dataset satisfied these two criteria. Table 8.2 shows the descriptive statistics for the four measures. The large difference between the mean and median for these variables indicates that they are heavily skewed. The skew can be largely corrected for downloads and page views by applying a log transformation, as shown by the histograms of these measures in Figure 8.2. However, the other two variables remain heavily skewed even with such a transformation. (The skew in developer counts is even more pronounced for the entire dataset, so it is not a result of the sampling.)

Table 8.2   **Descriptive statistics for selected effectiveness measures**

Variable	Mean	Median	Standard deviation
downloads	138,818.4	5,316.5	1,225,832
log downloads	3.68	3.73	1.17
page views	868,641.2	46,131.5	8,643,556
log page views + 1	4.62	4.66	1.18
developers	15.87	12	16.02
log developers	1.12	1.08	0.22
unique message authentication	6.67	1	23.68
log unique message authentication + 1	0.54	0.30	0.40

N = 2,168

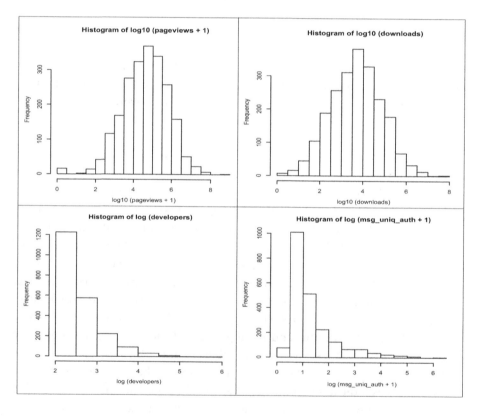

Figure 8.2   **Distributions of selected variables (log transformed)**

We next examine the relation among these variables. Because the data are not normally distributed, we examined the relation using non-parametric correlation, namely Spearman's R (results using Kendall's tau are similar). The correlations are shown in Table 8.3. These correlations suggest that downloads and page views are closely related, so both indicate a project's overall popularity. Interestingly, the level of participation in the messages seems to be more closely related to popularity than to the number of developers, suggesting this measure as a way to gauge the broader community around a project.

For comparison, Table 8.4 shows the correlations calculated for the entire dataset. The correlation for downloads is about the same, but note that including all projects boosts the correlation between the number of developers and number of posters of messages, likely because of the large number of projects scoring very low on both measures. This result underscores the importance of developing a sample that properly captures the phenomenon of interest (in our case, distributed software development rather than simply creation of a SourceForge project).

Table 8.3   **Spearman's R correlations among variables for active projects**

	Downloads	Page views	Developers
page views	0.75		
developers	0.21	0.25	
unique message authentication	0.30	0.28	0.06

N = 2,168

Table 8.4   **Spearman's R correlations among variables for all projects**

	Downloads	Page views	Developers
page views	0.74		
developers	0.18	0.33	
unique message authentication	0.29	0.35	0.22

N = 65,070

Case Study

In this section we present an example of how these measures might be used to compare the effectiveness of projects as a dependent variable in a study. We compare six FLOSS projects chosen to allow for meaningful comparisons. First, we controlled for topic. Projects within a single topic category are potential competitors so making comparisons of outcomes such as downloads between these projects valid. Second, to minimize unwanted variance, we chose projects that are roughly similar in age and status (production/stable). Projects at this stage have relatively developed membership and sufficient team history, yet the software code still has room for improvement, which enables us to observe rich team interaction processes. On the other hand, we wanted to have projects at different levels of complexity to provide for variability. Accordingly we picked three projects that develop enterprise resource planning (ERP) systems (Compiere, WebERP, and Apache OFBiz) and three teams that develop Instant Messenger (IM) clients (Gaim, aMSN, and Fire). ERP projects are more complex than IM projects since they have to address many external constraints such as accounting rules and legal reporting requirements.

The array of measures presented in Figure 8.3 and Figure 8.4 use data collected by the FLOSSmole project (Howison et al. 2006) from the project establishment in SourceForge until around March 2006. Note that we have taken advantage of the rich data available to show the evolution of these measures over time, rather than comparing all time measures. This comparison suggests that the most effective IM project is Gaim, followed by aMSN, then Fire, and the most effective ERP project is Compiere followed by OFBiz then WebERP. Further study can then address the question of what practices adopted by these different projects seem to be related to these differences in effectiveness. For example, what (if anything) are Gaim developers doing that makes the project more attractive to other developers or the resulting program more attractive to users?

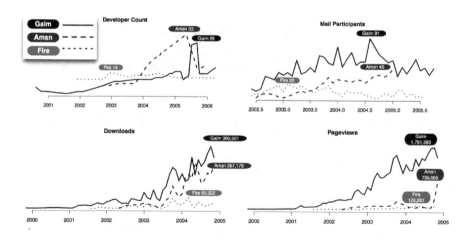

Figure 8.3   Comparison of effectiveness measures for IM projects

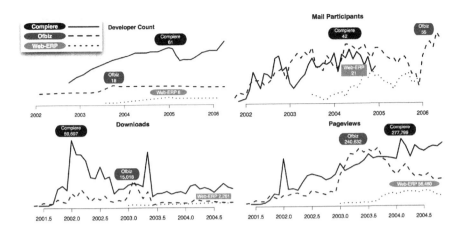

Figure 8.4   Comparison of effectiveness measures for ERP projects

Conclusions

This chapter makes a contribution to the developing body of empirical research on FLOSS by identifying a collection of success measures that might be applied to FLOSS. We have collected data on four possible measures for a set of SourceForge projects and shown the relations among these measures. The four measures applied in this chapter all have face validity as indicators. We emphasize again that we do not view any single measure as the final word on success. The moderate correlation among these measures indicates a degree of convergent validity, but as the measures draw on different aspects of the development process, they offer different perspectives on the process. Including multiple measures in a portfolio should provide a better assessment of the effectiveness of each project.

Most of the constructs considered in this chapter can be represented as cumulative variables, as in the large sample study above, or as time-series, as in our case study above. Even though the required analyses are more complex, there are clear reasons to prefer the time-series representation over the cumulative representation, especially as analysis moves to understanding the sources of project effectiveness. The underlying logic here is that the practices and structures reflected in the effectiveness measures may need to vary over time if projects are to successfully meet the challenges of different phases of the project's development (e.g., Rajlich and B.K.H. 2000). For example, initially it may be important to have a quite small group of developers, who can lay down a coordinated and consistently designed artifact, perhaps with appropriate modularity. Later, that small-team design may be better able to support a larger and rapidly growing group of developers (Senyard and Michlmayr 2004; Parnas et al. 1981). If such processes are at play, different measures may be appropriate for projects at different stages of growth. Furthermore there may be multiple routes to eventual success, and clustering time-series is a useful approach to understanding such paths (Stewart et al. 2006).

Time-series also offer the possibility of identifying periods of particular interest in the life of a project. For example, one can identify transition points through techniques such as interrupted time-series experiments. These techniques make it possible to identify projects that appeared to be performing well (on a combination of measures) but then stall, or projects that appeared to have stalled but manage to re-start and return to effective operation. The path of aMSN's developer count in Figure 8.4 is a suggestive example, with two seeming transition points. Such transition points could highlight periods for in-depth analysis which may cast detailed light on project risks and effective coping strategies.

Having identified particular effective projects, our future work includes more detailed analysis of the projects. We plan to employ a theoretical sampling strategy to choose a few FLOSS development teams to study in depth. By limiting the number of projects, we will be able to use more labor-intensive data analysis approaches to shed more light on the practices of effective FLOSS teams.

References

Arent, J. and Nørbjerg, J. (2000) Software Process Improvement as Organizational Knowledge Creation: A Multiple Case Analysis. Presented at Proceedings of the 33rd Hawaii International Conference on System Sciences (HICSS-33, January 4–7), Wailea, Maui, HI.

Boehm, B.W., Brown, J.R. and Lipow, M. (1976) Quantitative Evaluation of Software Quality. In *Proceedings of the 2nd International Conference on Software Engineering*, October 13–15. San Francisco, CA: 592–605.

Crowston, K., Howison, J. and Annabi, H. (2006) Information Systems Success in Free and Open Source Software Development: Theory and Measures, *Software Process—Improvement and Practice*, 11: 123–48.

Crowston, K. and Scozzi, B. (2002) Open Source Software Projects as Virtual Organizations: Competency Rallying for Software Development, *IEE Proceedings Software*, 149: 3–17.

Davis, F.D. (1989) Perceived Usefulness, Perceived Ease of Use and User Acceptance of Information Technology, *MIS Quarterly*, 13: 319–40.

Davis, A.M. (1990) *Software Requirements Analysis and Specification.* Englewood Cliffs, NJ: Prentice-Hall.

DeLone, W.H. and McLean, E.R. (1992) Information Systems Success: The Quest for the Dependent Variable, *Information Systems Research*, 3: 60–95.

DeLone, W.H. and McLean, E.R. (2002) Information Systems Success Revisited. Presented at Proceedings of the 35th Hawaii International Conference on System Sciences (HICSS-35, January 7–10), Waikoloa, Hawaii.

DeLone, W.H. and McLean, E.R. (2003) The DeLone and McLean Model of Information Systems Success: a Ten-year Update, *J. Manage. Inform. Syst.*, 19: 9–30.

Ewusi-Mensah, K. (1997) Critical Issues in Abandoned Information Systems Development Projects, *Communication of the ACM*, 40: 74–80.

Ghosh, R.A. (2002) Free/Libre and Open Source Software: Survey and Study. Report of the FLOSS Workshop on Advancing the Research Agenda on Free/Open Source Software, online document. http://www.flossproject.org/report/FLOSS_Final5all.pdf. Last accessed on October 19 2010.

Gorton, I. and Liu, A. (2002) Software Component Quality Assessment in Practice: Successes and Practical Impediments. In *Proceedings of the 24th International Conference on Software Engineering (ICSE).* May. Orlando, FL: Association for Computing Machinery (ACM) Press, 555–8.

Grant, R.M. (1996) Toward a Knowledge-based Theory of the Firm, *Strategic Management Journal*, 17: 109–22.

Guinan, P.J., Cooprider, J.G. and Faraj, S. (1998) Enabling Software Development Team Performance During Requirements Definition: A Behavioral Versus Technical Approach, *Inf. Syst. Res.*, 9: 101–25.

Hann, I.-H., Roberts, J., Slaughter, S. and Fielding, R. (2002) Economic Incentives for Participating in Open Source Software Projects, In *Proceedings of the Twenty-Third International Conference on Information Systems*, Seattle WA: 365–72.

Hertel, G., Niedner, S. and Herrmann, S. (n.d.) Motivation of Software Developers in Open Source Projects: An Internet-based Survey of Contributors to the Linux Kernel. Kiel, Germany: University of Kiel.

Howison, J. Conklin, M. and Crowston, K. (2006) FLOSSmole: A Collaborative Repository for FLOSS Research Data and Analyses, *International Journal of Information Technology and Web Engineering*, 1: 17–26.

Jackson, M. (1995) Software Requirements and Specifications: Practice, Principles, and Prejudices. Boston, MA: Addison-Wesley.

Kelty, C. (2001) Free Software/Free Science, First Monday, 6(12). http://firstmonday.org/issues/issue6_12/kelty/index.html. Last accessed October 19 2010.

Krishnamurthy, S. (2002). Cave or Community? An Empirical Examination of 100 Mature Open Source Projects. First Monday, 7(6). http://131.193.153.231/www/issues/issue7_6/krishnamurthy/index.html. Last accessed on October 19 2010.

Lerner, J. and Tirole, J. (2002). The Scope of Open Source Licensing, working papers, http://idei.fr/doc/wp/2003/scope_open_source.pdf . Last accessed on October 19 2010.

Mishra, B., Prasad, A. and Raghunathan, S. (2002) Quality and Profits Under Open Source Versus Closed Source. In Proceedings of the Twenty-Third International Conference on Information Systems: December, Barcelona, Spain.

Mockus, A., Fielding, R.T. and Herbsleb, J.D. (2000) A Case Study of Open Source Software Development: The Apache Server. Presented at Proceedings of the International Conference on Software Engineering (ICSE'2000). June, Limerick, Ireland.

Parnas, D.L., Clements, P.C. and Weiss, D.M. (1981) The Modular Structure of Complex Systems, IEEE Transactions on Software Engineering, 11: 259–66.

Rajlich, V.T. and B.K.H. (2000) A Staged Model for the Software Life Cycle, IEEE Computer, 33: 66–71.

Raymond, E.S. (1998) The Cathedral and the Bazaar, First Monday, 3,3. http://www.catb.org/~esr/writings/cathedral-bazaar/cathedral-bazaar/. Last accessed October 19 2010.

Scacchi, W. (2002a) Software Development Practices in Open Software Development Communities: A Comparative Case Study. Position paper for the 1st workshop on Open Source Software Engineering, Toronto, Ontario. http://opensource.ucc.ie/icse2001/scacchi.pdf. Last accessed October 19 2010.

Scacchi, W. (2002b) Understanding the Requirements for Developing Open Source Software Systems, IEE Proceedings Software, 149: 24–39.

Seddon, P.B. (1997) A Respecification and Extension of the DeLone and McLean Model of IS Success, Information Systems Research, 8: 240–53.

Senyard A. and Michlmayr, M. (2004) How to Have a Successful Free Software Project. In Proceedings of the 11th Asia-Pacific Software Engineering Conference (APSEC 2004), 30 November–3 December, Busan Korea: 84–91.

Shenhar, A.J., Dvir, D., Levy, O. and Maltz, A.C. (2001) Project Success: A Multidimensional Strategic Concept, Long Range Planning, 34: 699–725.

Stamelos, I., Angelis, L. Oikonomou, A. and Bleris, G.L. (2002) Code Quality Analysis in Open Source Software Development, *Information Systems Journal,* 12: 43–60.

Stewart, K.J. and Ammeter, T. (2002) An Exploratory Study of Factors Influencing the Level of Vitality and Popularity of Open Source Projects. In L. Applegate, R.Galliers, and J.I. DeGross (eds), *Proceedings of the Twenty-Third International Conference on Information Systems.* Barcelona, Spain: 853–7.

Stewart, K.J., Darcy, D.P. and Daniel, S. (2006) Opportunities and Challenges Applying Functional Data Analysis to the Study of Open Source Software, *Statistical Science,* 21(2): 167–78.

9

Little Fish in a Big Pond: A Comparison of Active SourceForge OSS Projects with Very Popular Non-SourceForge OSS Projects

Austen Rainer and Stephen Gale

Introduction

The majority of attention directed at free, libre and open source software (FLOSS) projects seems to be directed at the big, successful projects. For example, a recent O'Reilly Radar survey[1] on the most important open source software (OSS) projects generated a variety of responses, for instance Linux, BSD, Apache, MySQL, Firefox, Perl, PHP, Python, gcc, and OpenOffice (this is not an exhaustive or ranked list). These examples suggest that attitudes to the most important OSS projects extend across a variety of types of software such as desktop applications (e.g. OpenOffice, Firefox), server applications (e.g. MySQL, Apache), operating systems (Linux, BSD) and development tools (e.g. Perl, gcc).

Many of these well-known, successful, big projects did not begin in that way, but were started by individuals or small groups, progressed incrementally and opportunistically and over time they became well-known, successful and important projects and software. This bottom-up approach was partly

---

1 http://radar.oreilly.com/archives/2007/01/survey_three_mo.html, posted on 23 January 2007 by Nat Torkington.

a result of the (im)maturity of the open source community at the time. In more recent years, open source software has become well established and very well organised as indicated by, for example, the Apache Foundation, the development and marketing of Firefox, and the commitment of corporations such as IBM, Hewlett Packard and Sun Microsystems to open source software.

Despite the increasing maturity and organisation of the global open source community, there are still many small, independent OSS projects. For example, Krishnamurthy (2002) found that for the 100 mature projects he investigated on SourceForge, the median number of developers was four and the mode was one. Krishnamurthy found this to be consistent with results from the 2000 Orbiten Survey (Ghosh and Prakash, 2000): i.e. of the top 100 most prolific contributors, 70 were individuals or very small groups. Krishnamurthy's findings are also consistent with our more recent work (Rainer and Gale, 2005a): for 50,000 projects we analysed from SourceForge, the median and modal number of developers was one; by contrast, we found that for a sub-sample of almost 500 of the most active projects from that 50,000, the median number of developers was five and the mode was two. Ghosh, Robles and Glott (2002) have found similar results in their study of FLOSS projects.

In addition to the number of developers on a FLOSS project, there is also the issue of the organisation of those developers. Crowston and Howison (2005) recognise a number of metaphors in the literature to describe the organisation of FLOSS projects, e.g. Eric Raymond's *Cathedral and the Bazaar*, and Alan Cox's *Town Council* and *Clique*. For Crowston and Howison, project organisation is closely linked to social structure. Furthermore, it is important to determine whether there is a consistent social structure for FLOSS projects because this structure would help to define the boundaries of the phenomenon to be studied, but also legitimise the study of FLOSS projects as a phenomenon in its own right, rather than a subset of a more generic phenomenon of, for example, 'software engineering practices'. Rather than investigating code development, Crowston and Howison investigate the bug-fixing process and conclude from their study that a particular pattern of communications centralisation or decentralisation is *not* a characteristic of FLOSS projects when engaged in the task of bug fixing. They go on to state that it should therefore not be taken for granted that FLOSS projects automatically inherit the practices and characteristics that have been found in case studies or in the projects on which the practitioner-advocates base their understanding of the FLOSS phenomenon. We take this statement as a motivation for investigating those small, active projects on SourceForge that have not been the subject of research and have, therefore, not been explicitly represented in previous case studies and surveys. Furthermore, we think that it is important to raise awareness, amongst the researcher and practitioner communities, of these kinds of projects. For example:

- When evaluating which OSS software tools and products to adopt or contribute to, IT managers and developers could benefit from a set of criteria for helping them to assess the capabilities and potential of OSS projects. These criteria could complement other OSS evaluation frameworks, such as the Nonprofit Open Source Initiative's (NOSI) primer on choosing and using free and open source software (Murrain, 2003), and OSS Watch's Business Readiness Rating (BRR).[2]

- Teachers and instructors could benefit from criteria for identifying successful small OSS projects so that they can identify case studies or action research opportunities for students in their taught programmes. For example, Carrington and Kim (2003) discuss their use of several OSS development tools for student projects on a one-semester introductory course to software design and testing.

- Academics could benefit from criteria for identifying OSS projects that would be candidates for innovative research projects.

To investigate the 'success' of these small OSS projects, we previously collected and analysed a large dataset from SourceForge.net (Rainer and Gale, 2005a, 2005b). Our research identified approximately 500 projects on SourceForge.net that were active across a range of activity indicators and were therefore more likely to be successful. Our measures of success concentrated only on activity internal to the project, and gave no indication of the external success of the project. In this chapter, we:

1. Compare the external success of this 1 per cent of SourceForge projects with the external success of 17 large, successful, well-known OSS projects.

2. Assess how this 1 per cent of SourceForge projects have progressed over the two years since we initially collected our data.

---

2   Visit: http://www.openbrr.org/.

3.   Propose a revised set of criteria for identifying OSS projects on SourceForge that warrant further attention from practitioners and researchers.

The remainder of the chapter is organised as follows: the first section provides background information on SourceForge.net and our previous work in this area. The next section reports on our investigations of external indicators of success for both the SourceForge projects and the 17 well-known FLOSS projects. We then report on our investigations of indicators of internal activity within the SourceForge projects. After briefly discussing the implications of our findings, including a revised set of criteria for identifying 'successful' projects on SourceForge.net, we provide a summary of the chapter. Appendices provide further information on the 17 well-known, non-SourceForge projects used in our analyses, and also further information on the statistical tests we performed.

Background

SourceForge is by far the largest OSS portal in the world and as of early February 2007 has over 140,000 projects registered on the portal. (At the time of our initial data collection, the portal had approximately 85,000 projects and we analysed about 50,000. As a contrast, Freshmeat.org currently has 42,250 projects.) SourceForge is also popular with the research community. For example, a Google Scholar advanced search on the terms 'open source' and 'SourceForge', restricted to the subject area of 'Engineering, Computer Science, and Mathematics', returns over 7,000 articles. As a comparison, the equivalent search for Freshmeat returns just over 300 articles. SourceForge.net has been subject to large crawls of the data in its portal. For example, Weiss (2005) has recently extracted data on almost 90,000 projects from the SourceForge. net portal and provided a detailed explanation of how such crawls could be undertaken by others. The FLOSSMole (formerly OSSMole) project[3] provides data on SourceForge.net projects, as well as data from other forges, i.e. Freshmeat, Rubyforge, Objectweb and Free Software Foundation.

Howison and Crowston (2004) have discussed the challenges of extracting and analysing data from SourceForge.net, and it is generally recognised that most OSS projects hosted at SourceForge.net are inactive and that some of the data provided through the portal has in the past been unreliable, e.g. due to the

---

3   Visit: http://ossmole.sourceforge.net/.

way that developers use the portal to manage their projects. Furthermore, even the active projects on SourceForge tend to be small projects, and tend to receive considerably less attention from the academic and practitioner communities, at least in comparison with the popular OSS projects such as Firefox, OpenOffice, Linux, Apache etc. Given the quantity of projects on SourceForge, the potential problems with the reliability of data, and the fact that many of the active projects are not well known by non-specialists, it is very hard to effectively distinguish between the 'successful' and the 'unsuccessful' projects. It is also hard to derive a set of 'successful' projects on the SourceForge portal which researchers, developers, managers or users can then consider in more detail.

We have previously (Rainer and Gale, 2005a, 2005b) analysed 50,000 projects hosted at SourceForge.net in an attempt to identify the more successful projects on the portal. We used a number of indicators of activity, summarised here in Table 9.1, to identify projects and 'successful' projects were defined as those projects that met or exceeded *all* of the thresholds for activity as defined in the table. It is extremely difficult to define project success, regardless of whether one is referring to OSS or proprietary software projects, and our definition is a working definition. In a series of studies, Crowston and colleagues are attempting to develop a more complete portfolio of measures of success (e.g. Crowston et al., 2003, 2004, 2006). Also, SourceForge has its own measures of success, in terms of 'popularity' and 'activity' rankings, but we ignored those as we want to extract a subset of projects useful for broad research.

Table 9.1   Indicators of activity

Indicator	Thresholds for activity
Number of commits	> 0
Number of files added to CVS	> 0
Number of developers	> 0
Number of forum messages	> 2
Number of forums	> 1
Number of mailing lists	> 0
Total number of bugs	> 0
Total number of tech support requests	> 0
Total number of patches	> 0
Total number of feature requests	> 0

Our analysis identified approximately 1 per cent of the projects from our 50,000-project dataset as being 'successful'. A further 10 per cent of projects were defined as 'code active', i.e. these projects met our criteria related to source code modification, but did not meet the other criteria. We recognised that our criteria were essentially measures of *activity* occurring *within* the project, and they do not provide any indication of the 'external success' of the projects.

Since our initial work, we have re-examined our data and addressed a number of data reliability issues. We now have a sample of 527 OSS projects which satisfy the criteria defined in Table 9.1. We have used this revised dataset for the analysis we report in this chapter.

For the 527 OSS projects in our sample we have constructed a number of datasets for this investigation. These datasets are summarised in Table 9.2 and Table 9.3. We explain these datasets in more detail later in this chapter; in particular we provide more detail on the 17 non-SourceForge OSS projects. For each dataset, we indicate in the table how many OSS projects are in that dataset. We distinguish between those OSS projects that use the CVS version control system[4] and those projects that use the Subversion (SVN) version control system,[5] as some projects have moved from CVS to SVN over the period of our analysis and consequently have data from both kinds of repository. SVN and CVS are both industry-strength source code repositories that developers choose to use in their projects. As researchers we have no control over which repository or repositories the developers choose to use. Repositories provide researchers with a non-invasive method for automatically collecting data on FLOSS projects and hence observing some of the behaviour of the developers as they work.

For some of our analyses we distinguish two periods of time: data collected for the period 2002–2004 and data collected for the period 2004–2006. This allows us to gain insights into how these projects are changing over time. We needed at least two periods of time to allow a comparison. We wanted a sufficient duration of time in *each* period to provide a reasonable amount of data to compare. And we also wanted to concentrate on fairly recent changes that have occurred on the SourceForge dataset. For these reasons we selected two recent two-year periods of time for comparison.

---

4   See, for example, http://ximbiot.com/cvs/wiki/.
5   See, for example, http://subversion.tigris.org/.

Table 9.2   Variables used as internal measures of 'success'

Variables	2002–2004		2004–2006	
	CVS	SVN	CVS	SVN
Developer				
Number of developers	Yes	Yes	Yes	Yes
Total developers	Yes	Yes	Yes	Yes
Common developers	Computed once for CVS and once for SVN			
Ratio of common developers to total developers	Computed once for CVS and once for SVN			
Commits				
Number of commits	Yes	Yes	Yes	Yes

Table 9.3   Sources of external measures of success

Source	527 SourceForge projects	17 non-SourceForge OSS projects[†]
Google search counts	Yes	Yes
Google Blog search counts	Yes	Yes
Google Scholar search counts		
2002–2004	Yes	Yes
2004–2006	Yes	Yes
Technorati search counts	Yes	Yes
Del.icio.us search counts	Yes	No[*]

[†] The 17 projects are identified in Appendix A

[*] Not collected due to a technical error during data collection

External Measures of Success

THE POPULARITY OF OPEN SOURCE PROJECTS

To better understand the degree to which internet users, software developers and researchers are aware of the 527 SourceForge projects, we conducted several internet searches on references to these projects. We searched using the standard Google Web search engine, the Google Blogs search engine and the Google Scholar search engine, and we also performed searches on the Del.icio.us and Technorati websites. To provide a benchmark, we also conducted a similar series of searches on 17 well-known OSS projects (a list of these projects is provided in Appendix A to this chapter). Care needs to be taken when conducting these searches and interpreting the results because references to names are context dependent. For example, a search on the word 'check', which is the name of a SourceForge project, will return a large number of results that are not actually referring to that SourceForge project. As another example, a search on the word 'wiki' (again, the name of a SourceForge project) will return a large number of results that are referring to wikipedias in general and not specifically to the SourceForge project. Also, the Google search engines employ 'smart' searching which ignores hyphens. For example, searching on the term 'a-s-k' (the name of a SourceForge project) would return results concerning 'ask' and 'a-s-k'.

To ameliorate these problems of context, we employed a two-stage filtering process. First, we included additional search terms to narrow our searches. Specifically, we searched on the SourceForge project name and on the term 'open source'. For the searches of Google Scholar, we also constrained the searches by year, to allow us to compare the search results with our SourceForge activity data for the periods 2002–2004, and 2004–2006. We chose not to search on the term 'SourceForge' as we assumed that references to the SourceForge project would not necessarily include explicit references to the SourceForge portal. (Of course the same risk applies to the use of the term 'open source'.) Second, having collected the search counts, we conducted statistical analysis to identify statistical outliers and unusually high search counts, and removed those projects with unusually high search counts from our results. The second stage of filtering combined statistical analysis with personal judgement.[6]

Table 9.4 and Table 9.5 present summary statistics for the findings from our searches. These statistics are for the SourceForge projects and the non-SourceForge projects respectively. A comparison of the averages, ranges and percentiles between the two tables all show that the values are consistently higher, and often very much higher, for the non-SourceForge projects (Table 9.5). This immediately suggests that the non-SourceForge projects are considerably more popular than the SourceForge projects.

---

6   Initially, we computed z-scores for the search counts, and then sought to only include projects with a z-score between -1.96 and +1.96. Assuming the data have a Normal distribution, this filtering should eliminate approximately 5 per cent (about 26) of the SourceForge projects. However, this filtering only removed six projects (1 per cent) because the data are not Normally distributed. Even after the exclusion of these six projects, we still had project names that were common English words, and these projects had unusually high search counts. Consequently, we decided to include only projects with a z-score between -0.3 and +0.3.

We conducted two sets of statistical tests to check whether the non-SourceForge projects were indeed more popular. Our two sets of statistical tests comprised a series of independent-sample t-tests that examined differences in the mean averages, and a series of Mann-Whitney U tests that examined differences in the mean rankings. For completeness, results of the tests are presented in Table B1 of Appendix B to this chapter.

Table 9.4   Statistics for the search results for the SourceForge projects[†]

	Google Web	Google Blog	Scholar 2002–2004	Scholar 2004–2006	Technorati	Del.icio.us
N						
Valid	508	508	508	508	507	508
Missing	0	0	0	0	1[‡]	0
Averages						
Mean	85770	89	32	37	40	6
Median	11400	5	1	1	3	0
Mode[*]	1020	0	0	0	0	0
Range						
Minimum	16	0	0	0	0	0
Maximum	1250000	4414	2570	3400	863	315
Percentiles						
25	804	1	0	0	0	0
50	11400	5	1	1	3	0
75	62250	31	5	7	24	3

[†] All values rounded to the nearest whole number
[*] Multiple modes exist. The smallest value is shown
[‡] There was a data collection error for one project

For all tests, there were statistically significant results and large effect sizes, indicating that the 17 well-known OSS projects (summarised in Table 9.5) are indeed discussed on the internet in much greater frequencies than the SourceForge projects. Our choice of internet search facilities allows us to provide further detail on these differences. The academic community (as indicated by the Google Scholar results) is directing considerably more attention at the 17 well-known projects than the SourceForge projects. Similarly, the more web-savvy internet users (as indicated by the Del.icio.us and Technorati results) are also more aware of the 17 well-known projects than the SourceForge projects. The Google Web and Google Blog results suggest a general awareness, among the internet community, of the well-known projects, and again indicates that in general users of the internet are discussing the non-SourceForge projects much more than the SourceForge projects.

Table 9.5   **Statistics for the search results for the 17 non-SourceForge OSS projects[†]**

	Google Web	Google Blog	Scholar 2002–2004	Scholar 2004–2006	Technorati	Del.icio.us[‡]
N						
Valid	17	17	17	17	17	0
Missing	0	0	0	0	0	17
Averages						
Mean	9338941	11592	707	637	8518	
Median	2870000	7090	403	332	6184	
Mode*	488000	1031	28	4	839	
Range						
Minimum	488000	1031	28	4	839	
Maximum	33700000	36984	2370	2830	33398	
Percentiles						
25	1160000	3699	183	100	2878	
50	2870000	7090	403	332	6184	
75	18650000	15003	1074	738	9975	

[†] All values rounded to the nearest whole number
* Multiple modes exist. The smallest value is shown
[‡] Data were not collected from the Del.icio.us site due to a technical problem in our data collection.

EXTERNAL POPULARITY AND INTERNAL ACTIVITY

We were interested to know whether the degree of external referencing of a project by the various search facilities provided any indication of the degree of activity on the SourceForge project. We distinguish between those SourceForge projects that use the CVS repository and those that use the SVN repository because these repositories provide the data for our measures of internal activity. Also, since we collected data for the period 2002–2004 and 2004–2006, we need to distinguish these periods in our data. Consequently, we derived eight subsets of the data, summarised here in Table 9.6.

Table 9.6   Summary of six subsets

Source code repository	Period	Degree of external referencing	Number of SF projects
CVS	2002–2004	Projects referenced by *all* of the search facilities	162
		Projects referenced by only some of the search facilities[†].	344
		Subtotal	506
	2004–2006	Projects referenced by *all* of the search facilities	162
		Projects referenced by only some of the search facilities.	344
		Subtotal	506
SVN (Subversion)	2002–2004	Projects referenced by *all* of the search facilities	34
		Projects referenced by only some of the search facilities	42
		Subtotal	76
	2004–2006	Projects referenced by *all* of the search facilities	34
		Projects referenced by only some of the search facilities	42
		Subtotal	76

[†] Actually, all of the SourceForge projects returned at least one search result from the standard Google searches, which is to be expected as Google indexes the SourceForge portal.

Having organised our dataset into the subsets we then conducted statistical tests to examine whether there were significant differences between those projects referenced by *all* of the search facilities and those projects referenced by only some of the search facilities. We found a number of significant differences for the SourceForge projects using the CVS repository although there were only small effect sizes. We did not find significant differences for the SVN projects. Specifically, we found that:

- The average numbers of developers on the CVS projects for the periods 2002–2004 *and* 2004–2006 were higher for those projects referenced by all the search facilities, compared to those projects referenced by only some of the search facilities.

- The average numbers of commits on the CVS projects for the periods 2002–2004 *and* 2004–2006 were higher for those projects referenced by all the search facilities, compared to those projects referenced by only some of the search facilities.

- The number of common developers (developers present in 2002–2004 who were also present in 2004–2006) was higher for those projects referenced by all the search facilities, compared to those projects referenced by only some of the search facilities.

- The total number of developers (i.e. developers present across the periods 2002–2004 *and* 2004–2006 periods) was higher for those projects referenced by all the search facilities, compared to those projects referenced by only some of the search facilities.

- The ratio of developers (i.e. the number of common developers across both periods of time as a proportion of the total number of developers for both periods of time) was higher for those projects referenced by all the search facilities, compared to those projects referenced by only some of the search facilities.

These results were significant for both the parametric statistics tests (i.e. the independent samples t-test) and the non-parametric tests (i.e. the Mann-Whitney U tests) for the CVS projects but not the SVN projects. We speculate that the sample sizes for the SVN subsets may be too small for statistical tests to detect a difference. There were small to medium effect sizes, and these suggest that although the statistical tests find a significant difference these differences may not necessarily be particularly meaningful in a real-world sense. But Krishnamurthy (2002) found results consistent with ours, i.e. that open source products with more developers tend to be viewed and downloaded more often. For completeness, Table B2 in Appendix B provides a summary of the statistical tests.

While we have a number of statistically significant results, we need to be able to provide some explanations for why the results are significant (particularly given the relatively small effect sizes). For example, we chose the Google, Technorati and Del.icio.us search facilities partly for convenience, partly for variety across the search facilities, and partly because these facilities are highly used on the internet. It is not yet clear whether and how our selection criteria for the search facilities can help explain the statistical results. As noted above, part of the explanation may be that there was a larger sample of data for the CVS tests, in contrast to the SVN tests, with the result that the statistical tests on the CVS data were able to detect a difference on the basis of a much larger sample size. This, however, is a 'low-level' technical explanation concerning the quality and quantity of the data. Such an explanation says little about the actual *behaviour* of the SoureForge *projects* and the relationship of that behaviour to the external popularity of the projects. In the next section, we discuss the internal activity of the SourceForge projects as this may provide some explanation for the statistical results.

Internal Measures of Activity

PROJECT USING THE CVS SOURCE CODE REPOSITORY

Table 9.7 indicates that there has been a reduction in the average number of developers working on the OSS projects (with CVS source control) from a mean average of 4.6 developers in the period 2002–2004 (median: 2.0 developers) to a mean average of 3.2 in the period 2004–2006 (median: 1.0). A paired-samples t-test shows this difference to be significant with a medium effect size. (See Table B3 in Appendix B for information on the statistical test.)

There has also been a reduction in the average number of commits from 819 to 530 (median: 238 to 33) and again a paired-samples t-test shows this difference to be significant with a medium effect size. Notice also the reductions for the percentiles. Overall, there is a suggestion that the activity for these projects is generally decreasing between the periods 2002–2004 and 2004–2006. One explanation may be that many of the OSS projects in our sample are moving from development of new functionality to maintenance of existing functionality and this may require less developer activity and less commits to CVS.

Table 9.7   Summary statistics for CVS data

	2002		2004		Common developers	Total developers	Ratio
	Devs	Commits	Devs	Commits			
Valid	524.0	524.0	524.0	524.0	524.0	524.0	477.0
Missing	3.0	3.0	3.0	3.0	3.0	3.0	50.0
Averages							
Mean	4.6	819.3	3.2	529.8	1.9	7.7	0.2
Median	2.0	238.5	1.0	33.0	1.0	4.0	0.3
Mode	1.0	0.0	0.0	0.0	0.0	2.0	0.0
Minimum	0.0	0.0	0.0	0.0	0.0	0.0	0.0
Maximum	84.0	18605.0	82.0	13956.0	49.0	166.0	0.5
Percentiles							
25	1.0	48.0	0.0	0.0	0.0	2.0	0.0
50	2.0	238.5	1.0	33.0	1.0	4.0	0.3
75	5.0	799.8	3.0	385.5	2.0	8.0	0.3

PROJECTS USING THE SVN SOURCE CODE REPOSITORY

In contrast to the CVS data, Table 9.8 indicates that there has been an *increase* in the average number of developers working on OSS projects (with SVN source control) from a mean average of 5.0 in the period 2002–2004 to 6.2 in the period 2004–2006. This increase also occurs for the median and modal averages, and for the percentiles (the 50 per cent percentile is equivalent to the median of course). A paired-samples t-test fails to reject the null hypothesis that there is a significant difference between means (see Table B3 in Appendix B).

A similar situation is also apparent for the number of commits. Unlike the CVS dataset, there has been an increase in the mean average number of commits from 675 in 2002 to 877.9 in 2004. This increase also occurs for the median average and for all three percentiles. The mean average for the common developers is higher for the SVN dataset (at 2.7) to the CVS dataset (at 1.9). Again, a paired-samples t-test fails to rejects the null hypothesis that there is a significant difference between means.

Overall, there is the suggestion that in contrast to the CVS-based projects the activity for the SVN-based projects is generally *increasing* between the periods 2002–2004 and 2004–2006. A paired-samples t-test for the mean number of developers between CVS and SVN for the period 2002–2004 finds a significant result (see Table B4 in Appendix B for further information on the test). In other words, there are on average more developers working on the SVN projects for the period 2002–2004 than the CVS projects. Similarly, a paired-samples t-test for the mean number of developers between CVS and SVN for the period 2004–2006 finds a significant result. Again, there are on average more developers working on the SVN projects for the period 2002–2004 than the CVS projects. (Note that these tests are only for the 78 projects that moved from CVS to SVN.) A possible explanation is that projects using SVN are still in a new-development phase, in contrast to many of the CVS-based projects which may be moving to a maintenance phase.

Table 9.8   **Summary statistics for SVN projects**

| | 2002 | | 2004 | | Common | Total | |
	Devs	Commits	Devs	Commits	developers	developers	Ratio
N							
Valid	79.0	79.0	79.0	79.0	79.0	79.0	67.0
Missing	0.0	0.0	0.0	0.0	0.0	0.0	12.0
Averages							
Mean	5.0	675.2	6.2	877.9	2.7	11.2	0.2
Median	2.0	76.0	3.0	113.0	1.0	5.0	0.2
Mode	0.0	0.0	2.0	0.0	0.0	0.0	0.0
Minimum	0.0	0.0	0.0	0.0	0.0	0.0	0.0
Maximum	49.0	7872.0	59.0	10640.0	27.0	108.0	0.5
Percentiles							
25	0.0	0.0	1.0	10.0	0.0	1.0	0.0
50	2.0	76.0	3.0	113.0	1.0	5.0	0.2
75	8.0	862.0	9.0	961.0	3.0	17.0	0.3

Discussion

FURTHER EVALUATION OF RESULTS

We will have greater confidence in our findings when we have been able to benchmark them against other categories of open source projects. Specifically:

1. We need to compare the *internal* measure of success of our set of SourceForge projects against the inactive projects in the SourceForge portal and in other portals. This will allow us to develop a greater understanding of, for example, the decay of active projects, and the ratio of common developers.

2. We need to compare the *external* measures of success of our set of SourceForge projects against external measures of the inactive projects in the SourceForge portal, and in other portals.

3. We need to compare our external measures with other external measures. Our choice of search facilities was on the basis of convenience. For example, the Freshmeat portal records information on the number of subscribers to a project which could be used as a measure of external success.

4. We need to further investigate the transition of OSS projects from using CVS to SVN as this transition can distort the apparent 'success' of the project.

We also need to compare our findings more closely with the findings of other researchers and practitioners. For example, Capiluppi et al., (2003) have investigated the project characteristics of over 400 projects from the Freshmeat portal. They found that most projects are small and have a small number of core developers. Curiously, Capiluppi et al. found that over 50 per cent of their projects had no transient developers (defined as developers who provide at most one patch in the development of any section of the project, or those programmers offering up to three patches to the same part of the code). This contrasts with our findings where our SourceForge projects have a low number of developers who remain on the project across the period 2002–2006, which suggests a high number of 'transient' developers. Of course Capiluppi et al. are using a different definition of transient developer to us.

TYPES OF OSS PROJECTS, AND THE SUCCESS OF OSS PROJECTS

In the introduction, we recognised the presence of code active projects on the SourceForge portal. In our analyses, we have focused on projects that are active across *all* indicators of activity. There are different types of OSS projects and these types may have different concepts of success. For example, a SourceForge project may provide a set of stable libraries for use by other projects. For such a project, it would not be meaningful to measure development activity within the project, but the project may be successful if the code is used in *other* projects (either on SourceForge or elsewhere). We also speculate that as the FLOSS community evolves so the large OSS projects will take on increasingly formal structures and processes (as already apparent with the Apache Foundation projects) and so become increasingly different in kind to projects hosted on portals like SourceForge.

REVISED CRITERIA FOR IDENTIFYING 'SUCCESSFUL' PROJECTS ON SOURCEFORGE

Based on our analysis of the internal and external indicators of activity and popularity described earlier in this chapter, we propose in Table 9.9 a revised set of indicators for identifying those OSS projects on SourceForge that warrant further attention. Our general guideline is that a SourceForge project should satisfy *all* of these indicators. We do not include search results for the standard Google searches in our set of indicators as Google indexes SourceForge, so there would be an automatic search result. Standard Google search results could be included as an indicator by raising the minimum threshold to some value higher than zero. It is not clear at this stage however what a sensible threshold would be beyond a value of one. Also, we do not include type of repository (SVN or CVS) as an indicator. Our analysis suggests that SVN is starting to be used by the larger projects on SourceForge, as indicated by the higher average developers and commits for the SVN projects. Against that, our analysis of external measures of popularity showed significant results only for the CVS-based projects.

Table 9.9   **Revised set of indicators for identifying active projects on SourceForge**

Indicator	Thresholds for activity
Indicators of internal activity	
Number of commits	> 0
Number of files added to CVS	> 0
Number of developers	> 0
Number of forum messages	> 2
Number of forums	> 1
Number of mailing lists	> 0
Total number of bugs	> 0
Total number of tech support requests	> 0
Total number of patches	> 0
Total number of feature requests	> 0
Indicators of external activity	
Google Scholar search results	> 0
Google Blogs search results	> 0
Technorati search results	> 0
Del.icio.us search results	> 0

It has long been recognised (e.g. with the Hawthorne Effect) that when people are aware of being observed (measured) they modify their behaviour. A risk of publishing these revised indicators is that developers working on SourceForge projects (or indeed other OSS projects) will then attempt to manipulate information on the blogs and tag sites in order to increase their respective project's popularity. Because of the academic peer-review process, search results for Google Scholar should be harder to manipulate. Against that, academics will tend to investigate those projects that they know and are therefore unlikely to investigate the less-well-known OSS projects (which is one of the motivations of our work, i.e. to raise awareness of these lesser-known projects). Also, academic interest in an OSS project may not match practitioner interest, but academic interest does provide some independent investigation and evaluation of the OSS project(s). In the future it may be that one can raise the threshold values presented in Table 9.9 to counteract attempts to artificially inflate the external popularity of SourceForge projects.

Conclusion

The majority of attention directed at free, libre and open source software projects is directed at the large, well-known projects like Linux, BSD, Apache, OpenOffice etc. SourceForge.net hosts the largest number of OSS projects in the world, but most of these projects are 'inactive' and the data on the projects can be unreliable. Nevertheless, there are many small, successful OSS projects hosted at SourceForge (and indeed at other forges). In a series of investigations, we have sought to identify a set of projects on SourceForge.net that are active and, in some senses, 'successful'. To date, using a number of indicators of internal activity within the projects we have identified 527 projects on the SourceForge. net portal. In this chapter, we have shown that this set of projects continues to be active and successful. There is some indication of a decline in the number of developers and the number of commits for projects using the CVS source code repository which may be explained by these projects moving from the development of new functionality to the maintenance of existing functionality. By contrast, the projects using the SVN repository (78 projects in total) have a larger number of developers and make a larger number of commits. This may possibly be explained by the continued development of new functionality. We have also shown that our set of 527 projects has received considerably less attention from the internet community, when compared to the well-known, popular FLOSS projects. On the basis of our analysis, we propose a revised set of criteria, combining indicators of internal activity and external popularity, for identifying successful projects on SourceForge.net.

References

Capiluppi, A., Lago, P. and Morisio, M. (2003). Characteristics of Open Source Projects. Paper presented at the Seventh European Conference On Software Maintenance And Reengineering (CSMR'03), 26–28 March, Benevento, Italy.

Carrington, D. and Kim, S.-K. (2003). *Teaching Software Design with Open Source Software*. Presented at 33rd ASEE/IEEE Annual Frontiers in Education (FIE 2003) conference, Boulder, Colorado, 5–8 November.

Crowston, K., Annabi, H. et al. (2003). Defining Open Source Software Project Success. Presented at 24th International Conference on Information Systems (ICIS 2003), December, Seattle, WA.

Crowston, K., Annabi, H. et al. (2004). Towards a Portfolio of FLOSS Project Success Measures. Presented at Collaboration, Conflict and Control: The 4th Workshop on Open Source Software Engineering, International Conference on Software Engineering (ICSE 2004), May 25, Edinburgh, Scotland.

Crowston, K. and Howison, J. (2005). The Social Structure of Free and Open Source Software Development. *First Monday* 10: 2.

Crowston, K., Howison, J. et al. (2006). Information Systems Success in Free and Open Source Software Development: Theory and Measures. *Software Process: Improvement and Practice* (Special issue on free/open source software processes) 11(2): 123–48.

Howison, J., and Crowston, K. (2004). The Perils and Pitfalls of Mining SourceForge. Paper presented at the mining repositories workshop (co-located with 26th International Conference on Software Engineering (ICSE)), May 25, Edinburgh, Scotland.

Ghosh, R. and Prakash, V.V. (2000). The Orbiten Free Software Survey. *First Monday* 5(7). Available at http://firstmonday.org/htbin/cgiwrap/bin/ojs/index.php/fm/article/view/769, last accessed October 19 2010.

Ghosh, R., Robles, G., and Glott, R. (2002). *Free/Libre and Open Source Software: Survey and Study. Part V: Software Source Code Survey*. Maastricht, the Netherlands: International Institute of Infonomics, University of Maastricht.

Krishnamurthy, S. (2002). Cave or Community? An Empirical Investigation of 100 Mature Open Source Projects. *First Monday* 6(7). http://131.193.153.231/www/issues/issue7_6/krishnamurthy/index.html, Last accessed on October 19 2010.

Murrain, M. (2003). *Choosing and Using Free and Open Source Software: A Primer for Nonprofits*, Nonprofit Open Source Initiative (NOSI). Available at: www.nosi.net.

Rainer, A., and Gale, S. (2005a). Evaluating the Quality and Quantity of Data on Open Source Software Projects. Paper presented at the First International Conference on Open Source Systems, Genova, Italy, 11–15 July, 2005.

Rainer, A., and Gale, S. (2005b). Sampling Open Source Projects From Portals: Some Preliminary Investigations. Paper presented at the 11th IEEE International Software Metrics Symposium, Como, Italy, 19–22 September, 2005.

Weiss, D. (2005). *A Large Crawl and Quantitative Analysis of Open Source Projects Hosted on SourceForge* (No. Technical report number: RA-001/05). Poznan, Poland: Institute of Computing Science, Poznan University of Technology.

Appendix A: List of the Well-known Non-SourceForge OSS Projects

The 17 well-known OSS projects used in our analysis are: AbiWord , Bugzilla , Eclipse, FireFox, GIMP, Jakarta, KDE, MySQL, OpenOffice, Perl, PostgreSQL, Python, Ruby, Subversion, Thunderbird, Tomcat, Ubuntu.

Appendix B: Statistical Tests

This appendix provides further information on the statistical results referred to in the main chapter. All tests were undertaken using SPSS v12. The results of the t-tests need to be interpreted cautiously as t-tests are parametric tests and the data do not conform to a Normal population. For this reason, we have also reported results of Mann-Whitney U tests, as these tests do not make assumptions about distribution and variance. For all t-tests, equality of variance has *not* been assumed. In the Group column of Table B1, a value of zero refers to the SourceForge projects, whilst a value of 1 refers to the well-known non-SourceForge projects. For the Group column in Table B2, the value of zero refers to SourceForge projects that have not be encited by all of the , external search facilities, whilst the value of one refers to SourceForge projects that have been cited by all of the external search facilities. In all the tables, 'SEoM' refers to the Standard Error of the Mean. The effect size (r) is Pearson's correlation coefficient.

Table B1 **Results of statistical tests comparing degree of external 'success' for the SourceForge projects and the non-SourceForge projects**

| | Group | N | Independent samples t-test | | | | | | Mann-Whitney | | | | |
			Mean	SEoM	df	t	p < 0.01	Effect size (r)	Mean rank	U	z	p < 0.01	Effect size (r)
GoogleWeb	0	508	85769	8886	16	-3.4	Yes	0.7	255	54	-6.9	Yes	-0.3
	1	17	9338941	2735242					514				
GoogleBlog	0	508	89	16	16	-4.4	Yes	0.7	255	31	-7	Yes	-0.3
	1	17	11593	2596					515				
ScholarOld	0	508	32	7	16	-3.9	Yes	0.7	255	253	-6.9	Yes	-0.3
	1	17	707	175					502				
ScholarNew	0	508	37	9	16	-3.2	Yes	0.6	255	451.5	-6.5	Yes	-0.3
	1	17	637	189					490				
Technorati	0	508	40	5	16	-4.2	Yes	0.7	254	2	-7.1	Yes	-0.3
	1	17	8518	2016					516				

Table B2   **Results of statistical tests comparing indicators of internal activity between projects referenced by all external search facilities and projects referenced by only some external search facilities**

Variable	Group	N	Mean	SEoM	df	t	p < 0.01	Effect size (r)	U	z	p < 0.01	Effect size (r)
					Independent samples t-test				Mann-Whitney			
CVS 2002 developers	0	344	3.4	0.2	182	-3.7	Yes	0.26	21739	-4	Yes	-0.18
	1	162	6.5	0.8								
CVS 2002 commits	0	344	470	44.5	182	-5	Yes	0.35	19877	-5.2	Yes	-0.23
	1	162	1379	177.1								
CVS 2004 developers	0	344	2	0.2	184	-3.7	Yes	0.26	20902	-4.7	Yes	-0.21
	1	162	4.8	0.7								
CVS 2004 commits	0	344	272.6	41.5	189	-4.6	Yes	0.32	20395	-4.9	Yes	-0.22
	1	162	946.8	142								
CVS common developers	0	344	1.3	0.1	182	-4	Yes	0.28	20536.5	-4.9	Yes	-0.22
	1	162	2.9	0.4								
CVS developer ratio	0	344	0.2	0.01	323	-2.3	Yes	0.13	20143	-2.4	No	-0.11
	1	162	0.2	0.01								
CVS total developers	0	344	5.4	0.4	181	-3.9	Yes	0.28	21097.5	-4.4	Yes	-0.20
	1	162	11.2	1.5								
SVN 2002 developers	0	42	3.7	0.7	58	-1.4	No	0.18	617.5	-1	No	-0.11
	1	34	5.6	1.1								
SVN 2002 commits	0	42	437.9	132.2	64	-1.6	No	0.20	591	-1.3	No	-0.15
	1	34	794.6	176.7								
SVN 2004 developers	0	42	4.6	1.2	73	-1.2	No	0.14	513	-2.1	No	-0.24
	1	34	6.8	1.2								
SVN 2004 commits	0	42	577	265	73	-1.5	No	0.17	478.5	-2.5	No	-0.29
	1	34	1126	266.2								
SVN common developers	0	42	1.69	0.4	47	-1.9	No	0.27	602	-1.2	No	-0.14
	1	34	3.24	0.7								
SVN developer ratio	0	42	0.2	0.03	60	-0.5	No	0.06	463.5	-0.6	No	-0.07
	1	34	0.2	0.03								
SVN total developers	0	42	8.3	1.7	67	-1.4	No	0.17	547.5	-1.7	No	-0.20
	1	34	12.4	2.1								

Table B3   Results of paired samples t-test of developers and commits
             for periods 2002–2004 and 2004–2006

Variable	Group	N	Mean	SEoM	df	t	p < 0.01	Effect size (r)
CVS developers	2002	524	4.6	0.3	523	7.9	Yes	0.33
	2004	524	3.2	0.3				
CVS commits	2002	524	819	78.5	523	5.9	Yes	0.25
	2004	524	530	62.4				
SVN developers	2002	79	5	0.8	78	-1.7	No	0.19
	2004	79	6.2	1.1				
SVN commits	2002	79	675	140	78	-1.3	No	0.15
	2004	79	878	197				

Table B4   Results of paired samples t-test of number of developers on
             project

Variable	Group	N	Mean	SEoM	df	t	p < 0.05	Effect size (r)
2002 developers	CVS	79	6.8	0.9	78	2.5	Yes	0.27
	SVN	79	5	0.8				
2004 developers	CVS	79	5.2	0.8	78	-2	Yes	0.22
	SVN	79	6.2	1.1				

Index